Surprising Destinations

A Guide to Essential Learning in Early Childhood

Mary Kenner Glover
Beth Giacalone

D1413875

HEINEMANN
Portsmouth, NH

Heinemann
A division of Reed Elsevier Inc.
361 Hanover Street
Portsmouth, NH 03801–3912
www.heinemann.com

Offices and agents throughout the world

© 2001 by Mary Kenner Glover and Beth Giacalone

All rights reserved. No part of this book may be reproduced in any form or by any electronic or mechanical means, including information storage and retrieval systems, without permission in writing from the publisher, except by a reviewer, who may quote brief passages in a review.

The authors and publisher wish to thank those who have generously given permission to reprint borrowed material:

"Winter Dark" is reprinted from *I Thought I Heard the City* by Lilian Moore. Copyright © 1969 by Lilian Moore. Copyright renewed 1997 by Lilian Moore Reavin. Used by permission of Marian Reiner for the author.

Lyrics from "Morning Ride" by Malvina Reynolds are used by permission of Morningstar Management / Amadeo Brio Music, Hendersonville, TN.

Library of Congress Cataloging-in-Publication Data
Glover, Mary Kenner.
    Surprising destinations : a guide to essential learning in early childhood / Mary Kenner Glover,
Beth Giacalone.
        p. cm.
    Includes bibliographical references and index.
    ISBN 0-325-00376-9 (alk. paper)
    1. Awakening Seed (Phoenix, Az.) 2. Reading (Early childhood)—Arizona—Phoenix.   3. Action research in
education—Arizona—Phoenix. I. Giacalone, Beth. II. Title.

LB1139.5.R43 G56 2001
372.4—dc21   2001024214

Editor: Lois Bridges
Production: Elizabeth Valway
Cover design: Robin Herr
Manufacturing: Steve Bernier

Printed in the United States of America on acid-free paper
05 04 03 02 01   RRD   1 2 3 4 5

for Joan
who envisioned this journey long before we did

Contents

Foreword

When I was growing up, I used to take the train from the suburbs into New York City. The trip was always an adventure, with constantly changing views from the windows and a variety of experiences awaiting. Sometimes I went with a friend. Other times I met my grandmother at Grand Central, and off we would go.

Surprising Destinations: A Guide to Essential Learning in Early Childhood is full of rewarding adventures with many destinations involving teachers and students. Mary Kenner Glover, a first- and second-grade teacher, and Beth Giacalone, a teacher of three-year-olds, collaborated in a yearlong buddy project and have written about how this experience enriched the lives of their students and empowered them as reflective practitioners.

Last year I traveled by air to visit Mary and Beth at the Awakening Seed School in Phoenix, Arizona. As we toured the school, I looked through the corridor windows into each classroom and saw children actively involved as lifelong learners. Some were creating structures with blocks while others were reading by themselves or with a friend in a comfortable corner. One class was performing a play for a buddy class, while in another room, a teacher was leading a literature study. I met with the staff members at the end of the day, and their enthusiasm about the cooperation and collaboration they were experiencing told me that adventurous learning was taking place in the school for them as well as for the students.

Surprising Destinations is packed with examples of Mary and Beth's classroom practice, embedded within a framework of multiple literacies: content, social, community, humanitarian, and pedagogical. Especially compelling is the way they present human interaction as the key element in each of the literacies. For example, in Chapter 1, on content literacy, as we learn about a science curriculum study on changing states of matter, we also read about strategies for creating learning buddies. In Chapter 2, on social literacy, we read of ways that an older buddy helped a younger buddy overcome his shyness, and others became better at conflict resolution. In Chapter 3, on community literacy, we are shown the value of rituals and routines in a family grouping situation and also read about how the buddies learned to appreciate and take responsibility for one another. In Chapter 4, on humanitarian literacy, we are told about various community projects that fostered an ethos of kindness among the classes and helped two older buddies assist their younger autistic buddy. In Chapter 5, on pedagogical literacy, we are encouraged to value our ability as teachers to reflect on what we do, as well as to value our students' ability to make decisions as learners.

Surprising Destinations is not only about the adventures of teachers and students in a classroom setting. Mary and Beth's commitment to integrate their teaching with their life values is evident throughout the book and is explicitly addressed in the last chapter. They know that their personal integrity is reflected in their interactions with their students and that they must continually consider why they do what they do. They articulate their shared views about teaching and learning, which include a commitment to an emergent curriculum, a holistic approach to learning, the importance of listening deeply and setting high standards, and the value of working collaboratively. It is clear that they are truly committed to helping their students travel their own reflective journeys.

Although Mary and Beth build a strong case for collaboration, teachers who work alone in self-contained classrooms will find this book relevant to their situation as well. The cooperative classroom activities and collaborative personal reflections can benefit all teachers who are concentrating on developing curriculum, helping students grow socially, creating a classroom community, encouraging compassionate human beings, or refining their own pedagogy.

Reading this book is a virtual trip to the Awakening Seed. It enables the reader to experience the joy, the sense of community, and the rigorous learning environment that I encountered on my visit to the school. If you want to reflect about your teaching and travel the track of lifelong learning with your students on route to surprising destinations, hop on board and travel with Mary and Beth.

Bobbi Fisher

Acknowledgments

Early on in our work together, a train metaphor surfaced. It appears often throughout the book. We would like to recognize those who laid the tracks, served as conductors, and kept us from running head-on into oncoming trains:

Joan Moyer, Professor Emeritus, Arizona State University, for recognizing the possibilities of our work together. She remains an important mentor for both of us.

Our mentors who guided us along our separate paths to this common destination:

For Mary: Erma Pounds, Ralph Peterson, Linda Sheppard, Maryann Eeds, Elaine Surbeck, Karen Smith, Caryl Steere, Carol Christine, Carole Edelsky, Pam Clark, and Chris Boyd

For Beth: Mary Glover, Eric Margolis, Beatriz Arias, Erma Pounds, Chris Boyd, Rey Gomez, Kathy Mason, Suzii Junker, and Chris Faltis

The teachers whose work has shaped our thinking and educational practices:

Ralph Peterson, for his ideas on community

Don Murray, for helping us continually rediscover our voices as writers

Ruth Hubbard, for her time discussing research and collaborative writing

Georgia Heard, for her inspiration through the way she lives her life

Shelley Harwayne, for her visionary work on the cutting edge of possibilities for how good schools should be

Ralph Fletcher, for his thoughts regarding mentoring and writing

Bobbi Fisher, for her lifework of supporting teachers

Donald Graves, for a lifetime of helping teachers and children know that their stories are important

Lois Bridges, our editor at Heinemann, for her vision, enthusiasm, humor, and patience in the making of our book.

The children at Awakening Seed School, who teach us every day, and their parents, who support our work and give of themselves to enable it to happen.

The hardworking and incredibly talented staff at Awakening Seed School, who remind us daily how fortunate we are to be part of a learning community where the genuine needs of children come first. At a time when teachers are under such scrutiny, we consider ourselves blessed to work among such a fine group of professionals.

Personal thanks to our families:

To our first teachers, our parents, for showing us that anything is possible. To our children, Hailey (Beth's daughter), Sarah and Astraea (Mary's daughters), and Zoë and Emily (Mary's granddaughters), for the joy they bring to our lives and for reminding us daily why we chose teaching as our life's work.

Thanks especially to Martin and Bill for their support and generous understanding during all the Sundays at 7:30 A.M. and other times we spent together bringing this book to completion.

Introduction

It is the second morning of the big sale. A blustery wind prepares to challenge the placement of every item on the table, as determined vendors—three- and four-year-olds and their first- and second-grade buddies—hustle around the playground searching for river rocks to hold down the tablecloth. Once the rocks are at their corner stations, the merchandise is carefully transported from the classroom and placed on the table for display. Children hover around, many vying for position as a helper authority to arrange the stationery, bookmarks, and baked treats they have worked so hard to produce during the past several weeks. When the first customers approach the table, they can barely reach the goods, there are so many sellers on hand. Sellers soon become customers as the older children buy many of the items, some of which they have made themselves.

By the end of the first sale day, most of the baked goods and note cards are sold and sales have surpassed the $60.00 mark. The sale could end now, except the sellers are relentless in their eagerness to see that every last item finds a home. By the second afternoon, after additional baked goods miraculously appear to be sold as well, just a few bookmarks remain. Toward the end, as the sale is winding down, Tati, one of the second graders, notices seven of the smaller bookmarks remaining on the table. She turns to her dad and asks, "Can I borrow some money so there won't be any little bookmarks left over?" Her dad hands over the money and she makes one of the sale's final purchases. Tati then turns to hand out the bookmarks to her friends. Whales, bookmarks, and children all find a place to belong.

The idea for the sale emerged from the preschoolers' ocean study. After learning about different species of whales, an interest grew in helping study and save whales in emergencies. Once the idea of adopting a whale was presented, there was no turning back. Website information from the chosen organization revealed it took $60.00 to adopt a whale, so four discussions later, the sale seemed like the perfect fund-raising solution. The children decided two days would be necessary to raise enough money, and they set the date based on when they thought enough products could be made to sell.

For the next several Tuesday mornings, when the two classes joined for their "buddy study" time, an altruistic spirit pervaded the room, with saving the whales in mind. The older buddies took on the project as if it were their own. While they set to work at their tables, balancing full containers of paint water and finding just the right size brushes, they filled blank paper with watercolor designs to be transformed into note cards and bookmarks. The community of buddy readers became a community of inspired entrepreneurs.

A Bit of History

The sale was one of many events that occurred during the course of a year when our two classes found their way to each other. It happened at Awakening Seed, a small alternative school in Arizona founded in 1977, where working with possibilities is a primary focus. Literacy, both in the traditional meaning of the word and in a broader, more human sense, lies at the heart of daily living at the Seed. An emphasis on nurturing humanitarian qualities such as respectfulness, kindness, and compassion pervades every aspect of the school and teachers' philosophy. What happened with this preschool class and their first- and second-grade buddies exemplifies the rich learning that has gone on at Awakening Seed since its beginning.

As part of the work in possibilities, a buddy reading program was established in the 1980s. Essentially, each class in the school teams up with another class to do weekly reading together. Each younger child is paired up with an older child, usually for an entire school year or longer. The original intent of buddy reading was to promote a love for reading, to model good reading behaviors, and to give older children experience reading authentic texts to an authentic audience. Throughout the course of a year, some buddy groups extend their relationship beyond the weekly reading sessions for activities such as exchanging valentines or taking picnics to a nearby park. Others just read.

At Awakening Seed, an emergent curriculum model is used. What we do each day, each week, each month, and each year is highly dependent on what appears before us in books, in children's everyday experiences, and in life in general (see Glover 1997). Curriculum decisions are often made in response to children's interests and passions and sometimes even in response to the personality of the class itself. Thus was the case with these two remarkable classes of children, who ended up being buddies in greater ways than any of us ever envisioned.

Our work was full of surprises. Although we carefully planned how we wanted to go about learning together, inevitably something came up that we hadn't anticipated. It felt a bit like having a birthday every day. We chose to call the book *Surprising Destinations* for this reason, as a reminder of the spontaneous and joyful places learners can arrive at when the curriculum and teaching practices support this kind of learning.

We began, as most buddy groups have at the Seed, with a plan to read together on Friday mornings. This initially involved fifteen minutes of reading in pairs or threesomes sprawled all over the floor with piles of books around, or trying out chairs and tables to see if this arrangement enhanced concentration. After some reading, many trips to get drinks or use the restroom, and frequent spontaneous wrestling matches in the library area, we came together as a whole group to read a story. When the book was finished, a discussion always followed with comments like three-year-old Michael's "That was a great book!" We anticipated the usual adjustments related to learning how to be good readers and listeners; what we didn't anticipate was the extraordinary passion for life both groups exhibited.

When Hopefulness Is Necessary

Yes, there were a lot of days when we both wondered, Why do we subject ourselves to this every day? On a regular basis we deal with biting, unfocused energy, arguing, and all the normal stresses all teachers face. We've tried not to sugarcoat this story and instead just tell it to you straight. But we also wanted it to have a positive tone, to be a story that is true to our view of schooling. We love teaching and being teachers. We get excited going to work each day, wondering what will happen next. Although our students often exasperate us, we appreciate the antics as much as the accomplishments. It is our hope that our appreciation shines forth.

Early on, we noticed that the two classes, both highly energetic, somehow had a calming effect on each other. Once the initial settling occurred, the children were able to stay focused on their reading with great concentration and enthusiasm. We discovered that both groups loved to sing and shared some similar interests. A few weeks into the school year, the first and second graders were in the midst of a science study of bubbles and invited their buddies to join them for "buddy bubbles." The two groups of scientists used large hoops to make gigantic bubbles, as well as smaller plastic bubble makers and other apparatuses made of wire, straws, yarn, and paper clips to send off a wide range of bubbles into the air. Children who were timid became bold risk takers. Bubble experts initiated the less experienced into the ways of bubble making.

The interaction was so successful that we wanted to try bringing the groups together one other time during the week, apart from the regularly scheduled buddy reading time. This occurred on Tuesday mornings for the remainder of the year, and much of what follows happened on Tuesdays. A more detailed description of this work is provided in Chapter 1.

Sure Signs of a Research Study Brewing

- *Children change while engaged in a particular activity.*
- *Children talk enthusiastically about an event after it has happened.*
- *Children request further related or similar experiences.*
- *Your experience as a teacher was different (you think about the event afterward; you're excited about further possibilities to expand or develop it).*
- *Your practice as a teacher changes as a result of the event.*
- *Intuition tells you something deeper is happening.*
- *You find yourself telling stories to others about the event.*
- *Everyone has learned something from the event.*

We also chose to collaborate because of our unique relationship as teachers. For one of us (Beth), it was the first year as a classroom teacher. For the other (Mary), it was the twenty-second year. Similar interests in reflective teaching, emergent curriculum, critical pedagogy, and teacher research made the collaborative possibilities too tempting to pass up. As notes accumulated on yellow sticky notes, we were in awe of the complexity we observed in the relationship between our two classes. It was evident immediately from our conversations about our work together that we had an opportunity for personal and professional growth that would never be available in the same way again. We had a chance to learn a great deal about ourselves as teachers, as well as about our students.

The Train Study

After the bubble success, other work naturally followed. Three-year-old Antonio was a train enthusiast, and his passion soon spread to many of his classmates as they followed him around the playground making train sounds, picking up and dropping off passengers at various climbing structures, and trading places to be the caboose (see Chapter 5). Mike, one of the second-grade boys, was also a train buff, so we thought a collaborative study of trains might be a good place to start.

We made an ABC book about trains (see Chapter 1) and began a yearlong effort to learn as many train songs as we could. We found books about the orphan trains and factual books about the types and history of trains. A video of Mary's dad's model train layout fueled the fires of interest, and from there we were off to new destinations as learners.

As work together progressed, we saw how appropriately the train metaphor fit for much of what we did. We began to see ourselves as teachers, students, and learners on a journey that was new and surprising. We arrived at one point of understanding to be greeted by yet another whole set of questions and wonderings.

One of the songs we learned was "Morningtown Ride," a delightful lullaby about children riding along on a train full of sleeper cars. The last verse goes like this:

> Maybe it is raining
> where our train will ride,
> But all the little travelers
> are snug and warm inside.
> Somewhere there is sunshine,
> somewhere there is day,
> Somewhere there is Morningtown,
> many miles away.

One day after we sang the song, we talked about the meaning of its words. Seven-year-old Anna said, "Somebody's always waking up on this train." As we thought about our study and our work with the buddies, we realized that, like the children on the train, we were also always in the process of waking up. Each new station at which we arrived broadened our understanding as teachers and at the same time gave us greater awareness of our journey as human beings.

Multiple Literacies

We began looking at literacy and how it comes into play in learning situations in which children of different ages are involved. We observed numerous examples of how children were becoming more literate with print just through the weekly buddy reading. However, the term *literacy* quickly took on a more expansive definition for us. We came to define it not just as the ability to read and write or be educated but more as "having knowledge or competence" (*Merriam-Webster OnLine Dictionary* 1999), knowing a way to *be* in a variety of circumstances. Literacy, in our minds, has to do with a deeper understanding of whatever it is we are knowing. We noticed multiple literacies at work and named the following categories, which were sometimes separate and other times significantly interconnected:

- Content: Content literacy includes factual and practical information about the world. It contains general knowledge about specific topics, such as different kinds of train cars or how certain animals behave in the wild. Content literacy also involves the learning skills necessary for becoming literate in a more traditional sense of the word, such as learning letters of the alphabet or how to hold a book. When we speak of a content study, it is everything that encompasses the process of inquiry, as well as the actual information itself. It involves learning to review information, solve problems, think deeply and understand, and make connections in the world. In essence, content literacy is the scaffold upon which all other literacies are built.

- Social: Our second literacy category has to do with learning how to behave in acceptable and appropriate ways within a group setting. It includes both learning to be a role model and also following the example of one. Social literacy is an ongoing process that involves a complex set of behaviors, ranging from how to listen to a story attentively to learning how to take turns when two children want the same book. A big part of social literacy is learning to take on the perspectives of others.

- Community: We identify the next level of literacy as community literacy. It is closely tied to social literacy and occurs when a group makes a commitment to becoming a community. It is an extension of social literacy in that the emphasis is placed on the group as a whole, rather than on individual needs or interests. Community literacy enables the individual to see his or her place in the world, and there is a strong emphasis on belonging and being a productive community member.

- Humanitarian: The fourth literacy we have identified is humanitarian literacy. It is a more subtle kind of literacy and deals with aspects of human development that are connected to spirituality, morality, and the inner life. Humanitarian literacy often springs forth from community literacy and is also a highly personal experience for some. It is a literacy that helps us understand our interrelatedness to others in a more universal sense.

- Pedagogical: Although our literacy focus began by looking at what happened with the children, we realized rather early that our collaborative work also enabled us to become more literate in our teaching practices. Through observations, dialogue, reflection, and critical thinking as teacher researchers, we experienced firsthand what we have named pedagogical literacy. Our different perspectives as a first-year teacher and a veteran teacher added a unique quality to this kind of literacy development. Pedagogical literacy is a process by which teachers learn to perfect their craft as educators.

In the pages that follow, we will describe each of these literacies and how they manifested themselves in our buddy work. As we reveal our own pedagogical journey, we hope that somehow it will be inspiring for others eager to venture out on travels of their own to destinations unknown.

One

Journey on a High-Speed Train: Content Literacy

The bell rings to signal the end of buddy reading in preparation for the group story. Noisy children identify books from their own classrooms and put them in their designated tubs, bags, or shelves. Books from home find refuge in personal cubbies. Several children push chairs back underneath the tables and teachers remind a few stragglers to remove themselves from the space where the chairs need to be. Pillows are tossed—literally—on their storage shelf and a teacher reminds one or two devoted readers trying to steal another minute with a favorite chapter book to join the group. When younger children are situated on the laps of their buddies or sprawled beside them, the story of the day begins. Today it is Gentle Giant Octopus *(Wallace 1998), a nonfiction book about a mother octopus who lays her eggs in a cave and remains there for the duration of her life—five months—without food until her young are ready to live on their own. The beautiful watercolor illustrations and sensitive text inspire a passionate concern for the mother octopus. At the story's end, hands go up to begin the usual follow-up discussion—preschoolers, as well as first and second graders, request the opportunity to speak.*

When someone asks why the mother octopus has to die, Beth replies, "Sometimes in nature things just happen this way." Unwilling to accept this answer, students present several alternative theories for consideration. Eight-year-old Brendon suggests, "She could squirt ink in the cave so that she could go out and an eel might see the cave and just think it was a regular cave [without eggs]." Anna, a first grader, comments, "A wolf eel might move in, thinking it was just a regular cave." Many voices talk at once in response to Anna's idea. When the uproar diminishes, three-year-old Sami speaks: "If she leaves them, the wolf eel will eat all her babies and she'll be sad." The discussion, which normally lasts five minutes, continues well past the fifteen-minute mark until talk of a hungry mother octopus and rumbling stomachs ready for lunch bring this day's conversation to an end.

There were days like this one when we looked at each other in disbelief, wondering how we'd made it to this scholarly place with children so young. What sequence of events brought us to this conversation in which a four-year-old and a first grader could voice their ideas with equal clarity and confidence? When did this group of children take ownership of their learning with such passion and conviction?

If You're Thinking of Setting Up a Buddy Reading Program

- *Be sure to pair up stronger older readers, or those with a strong self-concept, with younger children who are more active or challenging.*

- *Establish a specific time and day of the week for buddy reading.*

- *Offer guidance for the kinds of books that are appropriate to read to younger children (e.g., lots of colorful pictures, simple texts, predictable language, interactive books with flaps, pop-ups, (etc.).*

- *Talk to older readers about successful ways to engage smaller children through humor, feelings, guessing, emotions, and so on.*

- *Start with a shorter period of time, such as fifteen minutes to read together in groups and fifteen minutes for a whole-group story.*

- *Give the children a few weeks to get to know one another before beginning other work such as common projects like the train book or other more extensive and complex learning activities.*

Looking back on our year of collaboration, we found it began with intensity and continued that way until our last moments together as a group. It started as a simple experiment to try to settle down two energetic classes that came to care about each other a great deal. In many respects, our idea to extend our buddy relationship beyond reading once a week was a survival technique, primarily for ourselves. We both knew we were in for a wild ride, and we quickly realized we needed to find a way to grab their attention or it would also be a long and exasperating ride.

Where Bubbles Led Us

As we mentioned in the introduction, our bubble experience together offered important possibilities for other involvement between our two classes. Our discussions about the two classes became more frequent, and we noticed how much more focused and engaged the children were when they were together. We observed positive responses from many children and realized that time spent with the classes combined seemed to bring out the best in nearly everyone. Once we decided to try the train study, the early sessions working on the train ABC book revealed more remarkable potential. To get started on it, we first asked the children to write or draw whatever they knew about trains. Each group worked a bit differently. Some used an individual piece of paper for each child and sat side by side, doing parallel work. Others worked cooperatively and figured out a way to share the task. Anna and Brendon drew the trains and long lines for the tracks, and their younger buddy, Sami, added the ties (Figure 1–1). They talked and negotiated during the entire process. David, who was quite timid at the beginning of the year, sat and didn't draw at all. I encouraged his older buddies, Jake and Tre, to shift their focus from their own drawings to a more collaborative effort. They responded quickly and showed him how to draw the train tracks. With that small suggestion, David began a whole page of tracks and an expanded artistic career (Figure 1–2).

In addition to the preliminary drawing, we put together a collection of train books from the library and our own classrooms. We gave each set of buddies four or five books from the collection and asked them to look through the pages for ideas. Once they completed searching, we came together and added their ideas to a list on chart paper. Our list looked like this:

A—All aboard!

B—bell, baggage, boxcar

C—caboose, conductor, crossroad, coal, cowcatcher

D—ding-ding (bell), dining car

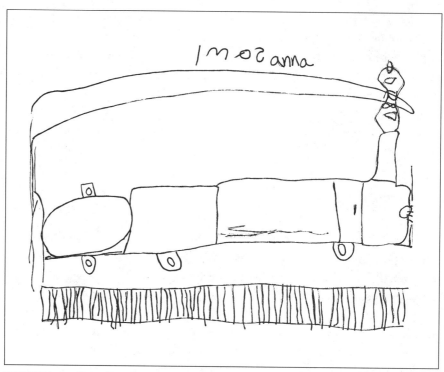

FIGURE 1–1   *Sami, Brendon, and Anna's Train Drawing*

FIGURE 1–2   *David's Train Tracks*

E—engineer, engine

F—flatbed car, freight

G—gravel hopper

H—hopper, hobo, handcar

I—information, Irish workers

J—Theodore Judah, junk

K—key

L—luggage, locomotive

M—motorman

N—navigator, noisy, Thomas Newcomen

O—oil tanker

P—park (train), people, passengers

Q—quick

R—robbers

S—Santa Fe, smoke, steam, station, sleeper car, smokestack

T—track, train, tender, tunnels, trestle

U—Union Pacific Railroad

V—valve, velocity

W—whistle, wheels, woo-woo

X—X (crossing)

Y—yackity-yack (passengers talking)

Z—zigzag (tracks)

Each set of buddies then selected the pages they wanted to illustrate for the book. Collage materials (paper scraps, construction paper, bit of cardboard), markers, pencils, scissors, and crayons were available to complete the work. As with the first drawings, the ways in which each group went about the assignment were immediately varied. Deana and Caitlin worked quietly on their picture of a train's bell. Deana, the older child, did all of the drawing, and Caitlin watched and colored in the spaces. Young Antonio was more directive with his older buddies. He made suggestions of colors to use on their train and said, "It needs wheels." Sami, Anna, and Brendon continued in the same fashion as with their drawing, with Sami actively involved in every step of the process. She wanted to hold the marker and do much of the writing, just like her older buddies, and they managed to take turns so everyone was happy. Alanah's log entry describes the system she and Mike and their younger buddy, Betty, devised to make their train pages (Figure 1–3).

Not all of the buddy groups were as successful. One pair of strong-willed girls could not agree on where to place the hair on the conductor. The older buddy, in frustration at the end of a work session, slipped Beth a handmade pink triangular envelope containing a blue note that said her buddy "did not behave very well

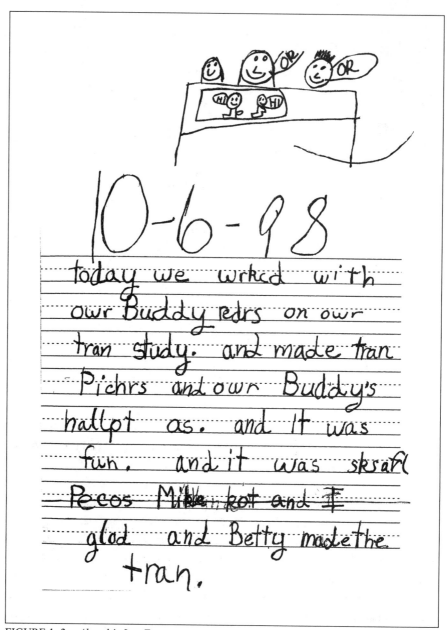

FIGURE 1–3 *Alanah's Log Entry*

today." Others wandered off for drinks or to play with toys, but for the most part, they worked very well together, considering how early in the year it was.

While some of the groups finished up their pages for the ABC book, others moved on to different projects. A few children requested an opportunity to make trains with blocks, cars, and small plastic animals. They made long trains of one-inch wooden cubes lined up with plastic bear passengers. Several buddy groups made tall, elaborate block structures that collapsed with a domino effect when a car or marble was rolled down them. Andrew described his block work with Michael in this log entry:

> *Michael and me started playing with the unifix cubes and then we started playing with the blocks and little people. We had a very good time because he was putting the people down a slide that he made and I could tell that he was having a good time.*

Deana, Tati, and their little buddy, Caitlin, made a structure that looked like a train track. They rolled a metal rod over it and commented, "It sounds like a train." An interesting outcome from this collaborative block play occurred the next day in the preschool class (Figures 1–4a & b). Their block play immediately expanded and extended beyond what it had been previously. The preschoolers created interconnected structures spanning the entire carpeted area. The block play was collaborative, rather than individual, and the structures were larger. Of course, there were trains in all that was built, including a station, tracks, and towns to which the trains could travel.

After we finished the ABC book, we decided to make felt train cars for the preschoolers to play with on their felt board. This activity, which involved making the train cars out of geometric shapes, was a practical application of the first and second graders' geometry study. While some children worked on their train cars, one buddy group spontaneously took all the scraps of felt in a tub and placed them on the felt board according to color, like in Donald Crews' book *Freight Train* (1992).

During the time period when we made the ABC book and expanded block-building skills, each class independently started learning train songs. Our common love of singing led us to begin our Tuesday morning buddy work with a train song or two. One day we made a list of all the train songs we knew. Here are just a few.

Some of Our Favorite Train Songs

- "I've Been Working on the Railroad"
- "Rock Island Line"
- "Little Red Caboose"
- "Freight Train"
- "Stop the Train"

FIGURE 1–4a   *Block Picture (November 9) with Buddies*

FIGURE 1–4b   *Block Picture (November 5)*

- "Morningtown Ride"
- "She'll Be Comin' Round the Mountain"
- "Engine, Engine #9"
- "El Trencito" (Spanish)
- "Down by the Station"

Throughout the year we continued learning new train songs and one parent of a preschooler wrote in Beth's end-of-year book gift that "the kids learned every train song ever written!" We didn't exactly learn every train song, but it was a rather impressive list by the end of the year. What we learned together about trains was a springboard for other work that followed.

'Tis the Season to Be Buddies

The next segment of our collaboration took us to the winter holiday season. We shared a simple Thanksgiving feast of bean tostadas and applesauce, which we made collaboratively (Figure 1–5). Before eating, we all sat in a circle and took turns saying what we were thankful for. Not surprisingly, one of the children said, "I'm thankful for the buddies." By this time, the bonds between our classes were growing strong. We were ready for our next big challenge.

Thoughts on Alternative Menu Ideas for a Buddy Feast

Bean tostadas and applesauce for a Thanksgiving feast? Believe us, there were good reasons:

- *We wanted to have a feast with items that could be made primarily by the children. Young children can easily peel and cut the apples, and it's a cooking project that meets the needs of a variety of levels of development.*

- *We thought it was important to have a nice meal for the children with the least amount of stress for us. Cooking a turkey and all the accessories is a lot of work!*

- *Beans and corn (okay, maybe not the salsa!) were staples of the native people who most likely shared the first Thanksgiving.*

- *We live in the Southwest, and some of us are vegetarians! Be sure to select a menu that fits the nutritional and taste needs of your specific group.*

FIGURE 1–5 *Alanah's Thanksgiving Drawing*

Each year our school has a celebration of the winter solstice. Years ago we decided to make the focus of the evening the solstice because our school has children of all religious backgrounds, and we thought the symbolism of the winter solstice—the turning point in the year when the darkest day begins to see more light—held universal meaning for everyone. On that evening, all of the children, ages three to eleven, dance and sing for the parents in honor of the holiday season. Traditionally, most classes work separately, but since it was Beth's first celebration of the solstice and we thought the older children in Mary's class might be helpful with their buddies, we decided to dance together.

Each group selected a winter poem to express through dance. Ours was this poem by Lilian Moore (1969), which we picked because it reminded us of the children with whom we were working:

WINTER DARK

Winter dark comes early
mixing afternoon
and night.
Soon
there's a comma of a moon,

and each street light
along the
way
puts its period
to the end of the day.

Now a neon sign
punctuates the
dark
with a bright blinking
breathless
exclamation mark!

Helpful Holiday Hints for Buddies

- *Keep things simple. Plan well, but don't get overly stressed if you don't accomplish everything you set out to do.*
- *Think of projects that children can do as independently as possible. Older children are quite helpful with younger ones in assembling materials, cutting, pasting, writing, and so on.*
- *Keep the normal routine in place as much as possible. If you are working on a special event, such as a performance, make sure there is also time for the familiar—and secure—daily and weekly rituals, such as buddy reading.*
- *Involve children in activities and projects that allow them the opportunity to give to others.*
- *Have the buddies make special gifts for each other so they can express their feelings and appreciation for each other through art and/or writing.*

FIGURE 1–6 *Winter Solstice Dance*

Using the ideas of the children, we choreographed a dance that began with the older children on the stage dressed in black, blue, or purple to represent the dark night. About halfway through the dance, the younger children entered wearing the same colors with balloon hats on their heads, representing the streetlights. Although the rehearsals were chaotic and not particularly promising, on the night of the performance, everyone came through and not even one little preschooler had stage fright. Everyone remembered what to do and we all felt like we'd accomplished a seasonal miracle when the dance came to an end (Figure 1–6).

Changing States of Matter

January is always one of those months when learning is at its peak. The holiday season is behind us and we can get serious about scholarly pursuits. It is also one of those glorious months in Arizona when we remember why we endure the summer heat. The days are mostly sunny and the temperature is just right. The weather and the time of year are perfect for outdoor learning. We decided it was time to blend art with science outside and make ice sculptures. As with the train study, Beth's class led the way. They made an ice sculpture one day out on the playground and the older children thought it looked like such fun that they wanted to try making ice sculptures as a buddy project.

Prior to the day of actually making the sculptures, the first and second graders conducted a ministudy of states of matter; the preschoolers did this as well, appropriate to their developmental level. The older students talked about everyday items that fit into each category. As a homework assignment, each child in both classes was asked to find examples of substances that were solids, liquids, and gases, and then the results of the survey were charted on large chart paper (Figure 1–7). Another homework assignment was to make the ice for the sculptures.

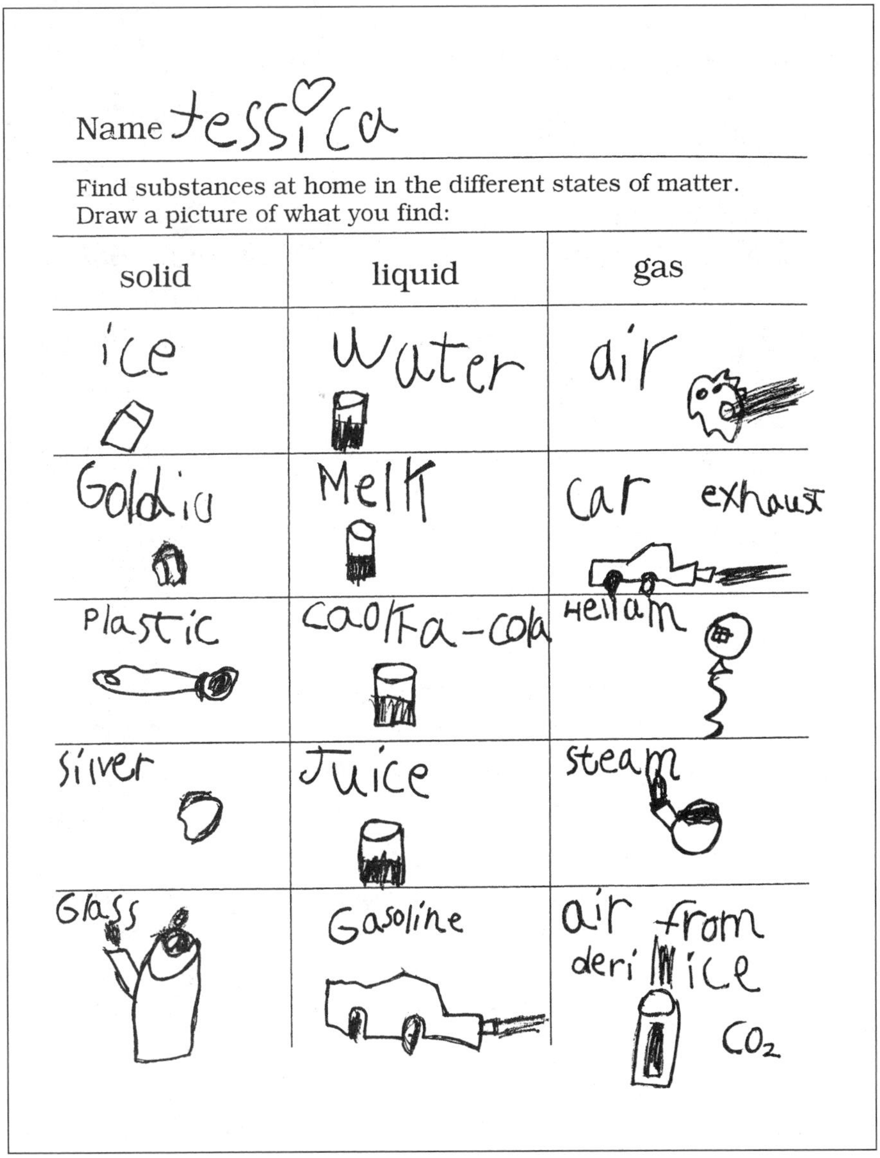

Name tessica

Find substances at home in the different states of matter.
Draw a picture of what you find:

solid	liquid	gas
ice	water	air
Goldia	Melk	car exhaust
Plastic	caolka-coa	Hellam
silver	Juice	steam
Glass	Gasoline	air from deri ice CO₂

FIGURE 1–7 *Jessica's Matter Sheet*

The children were quite excited about this. Tre, one of the first graders, was supposed to stay after school that day. He was so excited about making the ice that he called his uncle to come pick him up early so he could get to work on his ice-making homework assignment!

The day of the sculpture making, children arrived with plastic bags full of colored ice. They used containers such as bowls, cups, latex gloves, ice cube trays of different sizes, and molds to create a wide variety of shapes and sizes. Some of the

Some Tips for Successful Ice Sculptures

- *Talk about different states of matter prior to doing this project. Give the children as much experience as possible with substances in the various states of matter, especially those you can observe changing. For example, boil water to show steam, watch ice melt and think of different ways to make it melt, and list other liquids that can be frozen and melted.*

- *Make a list of containers that would work to make different shapes of ice. Some we suggest are ice cube trays, yogurt cups, plastic bowls, latex gloves, and plastic eggs. Send the list home with children several days before you want to make the sculptures.*

- *Suggest that the children put a few drops of food coloring in the water before freezing it. This makes really colorful sculptures and can be done in class as well.*

- *On the day you plan to do the sculptures, ask parents to remove the ice pieces from their containers and send them to school in plastic bags. Have large coolers available to put pieces in until you're ready to use them.*

- *Remind children to bring mittens or gloves. The ice gets really cold to handle!*

- *Before you start, have a large space—or several smaller spaces—set up for creating the sculptures. Although you can build them on the ground, we were most successful with small groups of children working on individual small tables covered with plastic.*

- *Be sure to have small containers of table salt or rock salt on hand to help fuse the pieces of ice together. And don't forget to bring your camera!*

- *It's best to make the sculptures outside, where they can stay for awhile. The melting process is as interesting to observe and document as is making the actual sculptures.*

- *Provide tubs of warm water for warming hands and cleaning up.*

pieces were no bigger than a fingertip, while others were so heavy the children could barely lift them. Most of the children added food coloring to their pieces, and some added so much that their ice pieces were almost black. We recommended that they bring gloves or mittens for easier handling. Once everyone arrived, we carried the coolers of colored ice outside and went to work.

For nearly two hours, ice artists young and younger fused together a rainbow assortment of frozen shapes by sprinkling table salt and rock salt on the pieces and holding them in place for a few moments. A few artists used more salt than ice for their creations (Figures 1–8a & b). On small tables, they constructed multicolor towers that balanced precariously in the winter sun. Some towers had tiny ice cubes encircling the top for decoration. Other masterpieces were walls made of red, yellow, green, and turquoise ice cubes. A few of the buddy groups combined their sculptures to fill up an entire table with one huge sculpture. As time passed and the sun took its toll on the smaller creations, one group moved its sculpture to the shade to extend its melting time. Eventually, nature took its course and the ice changed to water and later evaporated into the air. Nevertheless, the day of ice sculpting remained in our memories as one of our best buddy days ever.

FIGURE 1–8a *Ice Sculpture*

FIGURE 1–8b   *Ice Sculpture*

Dreams of Making a Difference

At our school, many classes conduct a study related to human rights around Martin Luther King Jr.'s birthday in mid-January. Our buddy classes were no exception. Although most of the work we did on human rights was independent, there were some interesting connections made between the two classes. In preparation for MLK Day, Beth's class read several books about his life and discussed why we celebrate his work every year. During one discussion, three-year-old Sami said, "Let's have a birthday party for him!" Seizing the opportunity to learn more about human rights within a child-initiated experience, Beth immediately began preparations. When the idea was presented to the large buddy group, Mary's class got involved, too, helping make paper chains and birthday crowns for each preschooler to wear to the party. The party itself was quite a success, and had it not been for a field trip, Mary's class would have joined the celebration as well.

While the preschoolers were working on their MLK birthday party, Mary's class examined human rights issues by focusing on artists who have made a difference in the world through music, dance, painting, writing, and other artistic expressions. Among the artists studied were

- Jacob Lawrence, painter
- Langston Hughes, writer and poet
- Diego Rivera, painter
- Jacques d'Ambois, dancer
- Sweet Honey in the Rock, singers
- Duke Ellington, musician

One of the dozens of books they read was Jacob Lawrence's *The Great Migration: An American Story* (1995), a book describing a series of paintings he did about the migration of African Americans from the South to northern states during World War I. The migration occurred primarily via train. This fact was particularly fascinating to the class after the buddy study of trains. During one discussion about the book, Jessica commented, "A lot of African American artists got inspiration from trains." Later, she added, "So many people were migrating. The trains helped them get to freedom; they helped transport them to newer and better lives. The trains were a symbol of freedom."

Ideas for Studies Focusing on Human Rights Issues

- *biographies of human rights activists*
- *Nobel Peace Prize winners*
- *artists or scientists who have used their talents to change the world*
- *voting rights (e.g., women, African Americans, Native Americans in U.S. history)*
- *U.S. history and violations of rights*
- *children's and women's rights*
- *current world issues regarding human rights (e.g., Chinese occupation of Tibet)*
- *examination of prejudice, stereotypes, hate crimes*
- *homelessness*
- *everyday acts of kindness we can all practice*

Note: *We believe it is important to focus on the positive aspects of human rights issues as well as the negative. For example, learn about the life of George Washington Carver and his contributions to humanity, rather than just learning about slavery and the Civil War.*

Trains came up in other literature studies as well. During a small-group literature study of *Baby,* by Patricia MacLachlan (1993), Jessica again made a connection between a book and our train study. While discussing all of the possibilities for why the mother in the story abandoned her baby on the doorstep of a loving family's home, she said, "Maybe she was just too poor, like in *Train to Somewhere* [a book about the orphan trains by Eve Bunting (1996)]." These connections seemed more significant because of the time we'd spent on the train study with our buddies. In fact, when Mary's class read the poem "Youth" by Langston Hughes, about the lives of young people marching along, Devon commented, "It's like our buddy study, it just keeps moving." Our study did keep moving in new directions and to new depths. The next phase took us to the deep blue sea.

A Whale of a Project

Around the time of the octopus discussion that began this chapter, Beth's class voted on a study of the ocean. We talked about ways the buddies could support this study, and one idea was to work on a large stuffed whale and other ocean creatures to hang in the preschool room. When we presented the idea to the whole group, everyone received it wholeheartedly. Mary turned to Beth and said, "Well,

> ### *Developing Content Studies with Preschoolers Using Their Ideas*
> - *Present the notion of using the children's ideas for study topics. Ask what they are interested in and send a note home to parents asking them to help the children write down ideas.*
> - *Have children bring ideas back to school two or three days later. As a whole group, make a list or web of related ideas. Arrange topics that seem to fit together into broad categories (e.g., farm animals, vehicles, occupations, etc.).*
> - *Look at the categories with the children and figure out which ones have the most potential, given the interests of the class. Narrow possibilities down to two or three topics.*
> - *Read books about possibilities for further information.*
> - *Vote!*
> - *Make sure to follow up on other topics of strong interest not chosen in the final vote. Ministudies of these topics help children feel that their ideas are validated and honored.*

I guess we're studying whales now, too!" As with the train study, we started by asking the children to search through ocean books and find sea animals in which they were interested. This time, instead of small paper, we gave each buddy group a poster-size piece of paper the buddies could draw on together in case they wanted to make larger drawings or paintings. The progress they had made as collaborators and artists since their first train drawings was remarkable. For example, David and Jake, who earlier in the year needed encouragement and guidance in learning how to work together, made some of the most interesting, detailed drawings in the class (Figure 1–9). They sat together quietly, both drawing, with Jake offering encouragement to his little buddy as he drew nearly a dozen jellyfish. He

FIGURE 1–9 *Jake and David's Ocean Drawings*

honored David's strengths and recognized them in his log entry that day: "My buddy wanted to draw a shark but he didn't know how. But it turns out [he knows how] to make a lot of jellyfish and whales and some seaweed." Amidst the tumultuous energy of our two classes, small things became huge.

Although Beth's class studied the ocean more extensively over the next several months, a huge project evolved in Mary's class that was important and exciting for both classes—the whale project. During our discussion of how to make the model whale for Beth's class, Beth remembered plans she had from Project Wild (1994) for making a life-size model of a whale. The first and second graders, who were studying measurement at the time, seized the idea and went to work on it. The original plan was to make a one hundred-foot whale, but after calculating the cost of the plastic from which to construct it, they decided on a thirty-five-foot gray whale instead. For the next three weeks, led by Mary's student teacher, Aimee, the class laid out two 35′ × 15′ sheets of black plastic, measured and taped a 1′ grid enlarged from the ¼″ original, and went to work making the whale. The children worked in groups, documenting the various stages of the project (Figure 1–10). Parents signed up to come help with taping the grid, numbering squares, laying down the big lines for cutting out the whale, and assembling it. Once the

FIGURE 1–10   *Whale Drawing*

Whalers' Wisdom

- *Make sure you have a large space in which to work if you're going to make a big whale. Outside areas work well, unless it's windy or dusty or too cold.*

- *Ask lots of parents to sign up to help with the various phases of whale construction.*

- *Divide the children into small groups so everyone gets a turn. Make sure to photograph each stage and have the children document what their groups do each time.*

- *Be sure to teach your students how to use standard measurement prior to beginning this project. We made a huge twelve-inch grid with tape right on the plastic from a one-centimeter paper grid.*

- *On inflation day, make sure your fan is large enough. We burned out a small one the first time around. It also helps to have lots of extra tape to patch up holes in the seam—we had many!*

- *Although the whale is safe to enter when inflated, remind children of the dangers of putting plastic items over their heads or faces.*

outer edges of the two flat whale shapes were taped together, we gathered on the basketball court for the inflation finale. We placed a fan near the whale's mouth, and it quickly filled with air. As children raced around it with rolls of tape to repair miscellaneous holes, the whale seemed to come alive. We invited the whole school to come see it, and everyone was impressed (Figure 1–11). Many of the children begged to go inside the whale, but we waited to do that another day. A thirty-five-foot whale on the basketball court was enough excitement for one day.

The whale project was a high point for both classes, especially the day we finally set it up in the multipurpose room and gave the children a chance to go inside the whale. They begged us for weeks to do this, ever since the first day we inflated it outside. Tati, age eight, described her experience: "When we went in the whale my eyes lit up in excitement." Classmate Julia elaborated: "It was gray and big. It felt like going into a whole different world and it is humid like Hawaii . . . When I got in I was so excited I was shivering but when I had to go out of the whale I felt like I was going to cry." We never really figured out why going inside the whale was so important to our students, but perhaps it was a message for

FIGURE 1–11   *Children Examine the Whale They Have Created*

us that even when children are actively involved in a process, they need to experience it all, from the inside out. Making the whale wasn't enough; they wanted to know what it was like to be the whale.

Although other ocean-related activities transpired during the same time period, such as making fish mobiles and the stationery and bookmarks for the sale mentioned at the beginning of the book, creating the whale remained one of the strongest memories of the year for the children. It was huge, just like the enthusiastic energy for learning that existed within and between the two classes. That energy gained momentum with the successful sale for the whale adoption and spilled over into other projects also with protection of the Earth and its creatures in mind.

We Made a World

April 22 is Earth Day and at the Seed we have a big celebration each year. This year we made a schoolwide art gallery to raise awareness of the Earth and its complex ecosystem. Some projects were done on Earth Day itself, while others were done ahead of time and displayed on the big day. We decided to make papier-mâché models of the Earth, so we completed ours during the week prior to Earth Day. In keeping with our yearlong tradition of working collaboratively, we divided the children into five small groups, and each made its own model. The first day, each group gathered around a table, dipping strips of newspaper into the mixture of flour and water (Figure 1–12). Older buddies made sure their younger buddies had a turn to place the gooey strips on the large balloons soon to be transformed into globes. After several layers of papier-mâché were applied and all of the holes were filled in, we let the balloons dry. A few days later, each group painted its model Earth blue for the ocean. The final, and most interesting, part of

FIGURE 1–12   *Papier-Mâché Globes*

the Earth project was gluing on the continents. We pulled out maps and globes so the children could see the shapes of the various continents. They sat at tables or sprawled out on the floor, working hard to draw their continents as accurately as possible. They naturally pushed themselves beyond our expectations, adding details we didn't anticipate. Brendon, age eight, wrote this log entry at the day's end:

> We made a world. And it was fun making it. Sami made Australia and that's the only one that I saw her make. And I made New Zealand and Tasmania and Taiwan and Indonesia. I don't like to do the more popular ones.

Julia and Mike not only did countries such as Canada, Mexico, and the United States but also included the Titanic in the Atlantic Ocean. Julia reported that "Mike did the Titanic and I made icebergs." Once the idea spread around, Titanics and icebergs showed up on many of the globes.

The Earth Day project was more complex—and messy—than anything else we tried collaboratively, and it helped us gauge how far we'd come since the beginning of the year. It was also one of our most successful activities, in terms of total student involvement, enthusiasm, interest level, and creativity. Additionally,

Papier-Mâché . . . What Were We Thinking?

- *If you have a lapse in sanity and decide to try papier-mâché with thirty three- to eight-year-olds like we did, keep in mind that it's a great project to do outside—or with a lot of newspaper on the tables and floors.*
- *Have the paper strips cut ahead of time; 1" × 6" is a perfect size for small hands. We had a table set up for each group of five to six children.*
- *Use white glue with water or liquid starch rather than flour and water. It comes off of the hairs on children's arms more easily and makes less mess.*
- *Have several water tubs near the tables to avoid trails of papier-mâché on the carpeting.*
- *If you're planning to paint your project, you'll need at least one other work session to complete the next phase.*
- *For days when you're short on math ideas, you can always count the drops of papier-mâché trailing down the hallway carpeting.*

the celebration in honor of Mother Earth set the tone for other end-of-year festivities, beginning with handprinted Mother's Day cards and ending with Mud and Sand Day.

Everything Was a Highlight

The hard work put forth for the whale adoption sale and the efforts for Earth Day put us in an altruistic mood toward the end of the year. When Mother's Day approached, it seemed like a natural choice to make cards together.

The children took turns working at a table with their buddies, first making two handprints with tempera paint on their papers, and then writing brief Mother's Day greetings. The older children were careful to write the messages exactly as their buddies dictated them. They asked for correct spellings for words like *beautiful,* ending up with greetings such as Tre's "Thank you for birthing me" and Clara's "I like you because you read me books before I go to bed and I love you." These heartfelt greeting cards were yet another product of children who cared about their mothers—and their buddies' mothers—and also one another.

As the year's ending came closer, we made lists of what we still wanted to do and what activities we thought were highlights. Each class made a separate list and then we combined them. Here are the two lists:

Ideas	Highlights
computer games	drawing and painting
drawing	sharing a buddy (with a classmate)
book of favorite buddy activities	ice sculptures
soccer	train study
math games	making the whale/whale study
Barney games	going to the nursing home with buddies
make cupcakes/cooking	going inside the whale
play cars	making cookies
smaller whales	Thanksgiving feast
build mechanical things	pizza party
dress-up day	globes (for Earth Day)
do a play with the buddies	bubbles
arts and crafts	playing cars/blocks
build a big castle or playhouse	horses and people
play in multipurpose room w/ buddies	read books

Not surprisingly, nearly everything we did was listed as a highlight. It was clearly an enjoyable year. After we assembled the list, we asked the buddies to illustrate their favorite highlight (Figures 1–13a & b) in much the same way that they began the year drawing trains together. This time, however, we all shared a history, and the interactions and drawings were more comprehensive.

Ironically, many of the suggested activities on the list for further work together were either variations of what we'd already done or opportunities to just play. It was clear that they loved the planned projects, but they also appreciated the chance to interact in less structured ways. A messy and muddy chance to do just that was our final collaboration of the year.

During the last week of school, the children in Mary's class made certificates for their preschool buddies (see Chapter 2) to bring an appreciative closure to the time spent together. Following the more serious and thoughtful exchange of thanks that went with the certificates, we went outside for Mud and Sand Day. The children wore their swimming suits to school, and we flooded the sand pile

FIGURE 1–13a   *Jessica—Cookie Drawing*

FIGURE 1–13b   *Sami—People Drawing*

Water Play Suggestions

- *Offer other options for those who prefer not to get wet.*

- *Provide running as well as standing water.*

- *Sand is good to play in with water, but sometimes it simply absorbs the water; dirt—or a mixture of sand and dirt—is great for digging ditches, tunnels, and bridges.*

- *Offer various choices of toys for water play to inspire imaginative play such as a shower from an old teapot and a hose, a kitchen and mud-pie assembly line, or pretending to put out a fire.*

- *Offer water play as frequently as you can—it is a wonderful learning opportunity that usually carries with it a great deal of joy and laughter.*

- *Occasionally offer a tactile sensation experience as well during water play (e.g., shaving cream, soapy water, or hair gel to play with while getting wet).*

- *Expect to get wet yourself—you will!*

for a morning of water play. They dug channels in the wet sand, threw mud balls (for a short time), chased each other around, and generally indulged themselves in the muddy madness. Some lounged on the climbing structures, pretending they were at the beach. With great abandon they played together, almost as if summer had already begun. It was a perfectly wild ending to an unforgettable year.

Two

Down in the Dining Car: Social Literacy

The classes come together on a chilly December morning for a joint field trip to a production of The Velveteen Rabbit. *After climbing into separate cars at school, they meet at the theater. Once there, the children fold into their seats, then immediately get up and move so that they can sit next to their buddies. They quietly chat with one another as they wait for the play to begin. Several larger school groups are late for the play, causing a delay in the show. The audience grows while most groups fidget and grow impatient. Not ours. We look incredulously at each other. Could this be our energetic group? They are the most quiet, patient children in the theater. Even the three-year-olds are calm—smiling, talking to their buddies, or chatting with one another quietly while they wait. Together, the children are able to do what many others cannot—remain content to simply be together.*

Apart, the classes were alive with energy. When together, a calm settled over them, it surprised us both. The older children magically became role models for the younger children, who looked up to them and wanted to be like them. When the buddies rushed to find a place to sit and share both loved texts and personal stories, they learned about one another.

They became close through these times together, sometimes making lasting friendships, sometimes forming simple bonds. All came away changed because of their interaction with one another. The changes took the form of

- prosocial behavior
- learning from role modeling
- personal growth
- friendship
- simply sharing stories with an acquaintance

Setting a Good Example

Preschool is a forum for social learning. Preschoolers are trying out new behaviors and strategies for solving problems, resolving conflicts, and learning how to deal emotionally with all the changes in their lives. They look to others to observe and imitate. In a buddy reading setting, the older buddy is naturally seen as a role model not only for reading and other academics but for behavior, negotiating his or her way through disagreements, interpersonal relationships, and stressful situations. Often, these role models are not at all attempting to teach their younger counterparts (Stone 1998). The goal in most buddy reading groupings is to have the older children model effective reading techniques. Other kinds of learning come by chance. In our classrooms, we make an effort to help the older children be aware of the power they have in their roles. We remind them frequently that the younger

> ### *Ways to Promote Positive Role Modeling*
> - *Give frequent reminders about positive behaviors.*
> - *Have frank discussions about how to behave when around younger buddies, giving lots of examples of positive behavior.*
> - *Point out ways in which younger children imitate behaviors of others (positive and negative imitating).*
> - *Discuss role models with younger children and what it means to set an example. Explain to them that they, too, need to be role models for other children and for their older buddies as well.*
> - *Make a point of acknowledging when younger children are doing a good job of behaving appropriately even when older role models aren't.*

ones will watch and imitate their behaviors. This, as well as the natural inclination the older children felt toward nurturing, created a warm environment in which the children were aware of their actions and the meanings conveyed to the younger children. This chance relationship between two groups of children led to further and more specific work on their individual social lives.

One day in class, three-year-old Sami watched as an older buddy roughhoused with his friends. Hands on her hips, she called out to him, "You're not setting a good example!" This became Sami's phrase whenever peers or other students weren't following school rules or directions. We noticed that the preschoolers, like Sami, soon began to own the language we used with the older children. Before long, the preschool students were overheard telling other children to be good role models while others asked their friends if they were doing their best. There was a shift in the way the preschoolers spoke to and treated one another, especially just after they returned from the older classroom. One remarkable change was in the way they began to allow friends to have turns before they took one. This practice was very different from the "me first" rule that most preschoolers make their credo. There were changes among the older children as well. As the older children learned how important their roles were, they became more aware of their own behavior. At the beginning of the year, two of the boys spent much time under the table, wrestling, or simply getting distracted from the task of buddy reading. As the year went on, they were able to focus much more quickly.

Ideas for Facilitating Conflict Resolution

- *Have children role-play. Older children can be helpful in presenting specific scenarios.*
- *Discussion and elicitation of ideas from children on what else can be done in real situations besides engaging in conflict are beneficial. Real-life classroom situations seem to work best.*
- *In preschool (after they have learned a few tools), remove the object that is the cause of the disagreement so the children can focus on problem resolution. You can give the object back once they agree to a solution.*
- *Older children respond well to participation in problem-solving discussions. They often come up with the most sensible and logical rules, consequences, and plans for resolving school conflicts.*

Early in the year, the younger class had a few incidents in which conflict resulted in hitting, biting, or pushing. The preschoolers brainstormed ways to handle these difficult situations and tried to work them out on their own. During these difficult few weeks, Beth also talked to some of the older children about the behaviors that were happening in the younger classroom. One of them was Tati, whose younger sister Theo was a preschool student. Beth mentioned that they were really working hard at finding ways to solve problems with words and not physical acts. Tati and her friends Deana and Melisa discussed possibilities for their assistance. Their solution was to come to the preschool class one morning and role-play several potentially difficult situations. In one scenario Tati held a toy. She said, "It is my favorite toy, and I really want to play with it." Deana grabbed it and tried to take it away. The girls pretended to get into a tug-of-war and screaming match. They then stopped and discussed other ways in which the younger children could solve the problem. They offered suggestions and asked questions about how the problem might be solved. They repeated the scene using the suggested method. The girls then role-played a familiar scene in their own classroom. They pretended to tease one another and exclude one girl from the group. This made Deana, the convincing actress, very sad and dejected. The girls again brainstormed with the class and amongst themselves for an acceptable and comfortable solution. The

If You're Trying to Encourage Prosocial Behavior

- *Help children see ways in which they can be helpful and include others.*
- *Introduce the concept of empathy. One of the best ways to move them toward prosocial behavior is to ask questions like: Do you like it when someone hits you or takes something from you? What might make her or him feel better?*
- *Encourage practice, in groups and individually, with problem solving and compromising. Ask questions like: How can we solve this problem so everyone is happy?*
- *Be patient and encouraging. Young children will gain a huge sense of pride and confidence by being able to solve problems themselves.*
- *Show appreciation and notice when someone does something great for others. Soon others will follow.*

younger children watched intently, absorbing all the wisdom the older students had to share. It was a turning point in the preschool classroom. The younger children became much more active in their own problem solving and, although not completely independent, they took more initiative in ending disputes. One very successful line the preschoolers learned from the dialogue with the older children became the saving phrase of the class. The children began to ask one another, "Can I have that after you are done?" Beth, her aide Renee, and their class, new tools in hand, breathed a sigh of relief. Beth and Renee had done role-playing and discussed these important verbal tools with the children before, but it was much more meaningful and was internalized more quickly when it came from the respected older children. It was a powerful reminder to us, too, that children are often the best teachers of other children, and sometimes our best move is to step aside and let them teach their lessons.

A Place to Connect

In the preschool class, four children asked throughout the morning, "Is today buddy reading?" The announcement "It is time for buddy reading!" produced a loud "Yeah!" even though cleanup, the least favorite activity of most of the preschoolers and their teachers, was necessary first. After lining up, little feet hurried down the long hallway from their end of the building to their buddies' classroom. When one child opened the door, the older buddies were just inside the door waiting for them. Sometimes the older children anticipated their buddies' arrival and asked to get a drink several seconds before the buddies arrived so they could see their buddies a second before the others. Almost all buddies greeted one another with a hug and a smile. When a younger child was absent, his older buddy heard the news, asked if the child was all right, and looked around intently to find another pair or trio of readers to join for the day. During every meeting, each grouping would hurry to its special spot. Often the space was cramped, with children huddling under a table or two bodies squeezing into the teacher's chair. They found the physical space where their emotional and literary connections were best met and supported. Once seated, many children could be seen sitting up against one another, touching heads together while reading, holding hands, or putting their arms around one another. Their touching communicated personal acceptance and a sense of belonging. It helped them settle into the activity of reading with one another in comfortable, easy ways.

Learning How to Be

Sami, a vivacious three-year-old, huddled next to her buddies under a desk. The buddies took turns reading. Sami, the youngest buddy, demanded a turn of her own. The older buddies never mentioned that she couldn't yet read; they simply listened and commented on the story being recounted. Sami beamed when she was with her buddies, and Anna was equally taken with Sami. Only weeks before, Anna had given Sami her play kitchen for her bedroom when she no longer needed it. Brendon and Sami arranged a play date at his house. The children were firmly attached to one another. This bond, which existed for many of the buddies, was the basis for much of the social learning that took place between the two classes. The closeness they felt made it easier for the children to put forth their very best effort.

Older children became more socially active as they tried to engage younger, less socially skilled children; conversely, younger children made an effort to use more advanced social skills because they wanted to interact with the older children. Brownell (1990) writes that mixed-age groupings are settings in which children can acquire and consolidate social skills. Helping, sharing, and turn taking are some of the prosocial behaviors that are more common in mixed-age settings. French (1986) says younger children look to the older children as caretakers, while the older children accept their responsibility for the younger children willingly. Together, these perceptions work to benefit all involved. We certainly found this to be true with our two classes. In particular, we noticed significant growth with a few individual children and/or their buddies that we believe exemplified what the buddy arrangement can provide for children.

Bravery and a Path Toward Understanding

Much of our attention with the buddy work focused on the group as a whole, particularly when it came to developing prosocial behavior. The playful spirit of the collective community and the support children felt within the larger group contributed to both a sense of safety and acceptance. Four-year-old David was a profound example of unexpected strength that emerged through playful opportunities in a safe setting. He was the oldest child in the preschool class but was also the most shy and reserved. At the beginning of the year, he observed intently while other children played, sang, and participated. At lunch, the social hour, David sat quietly and watched the others chat away. The first buddy activity we did besides reading was an exploration of bubbles (see the Introduction). David was hesitant to join in. With a little encouragement from Mary, David approached a large tub of bubbles where his buddies stood trying out various techniques. He tried smaller wands that worked but didn't interest him very much. Just as we thought he would lose interest, something magical happened: Tre instructed David in the art of person-size bubble making. David picked up a huge loop in just the right way. The sheer pleasure on David's face was enough to make us smile for days. David made bubbles, many of which were bigger than he, for longer than any other preschooler. He and his buddies laughed and talked and bonded. It was an awakening for David that began a year of unexpected personal growth.

In Chapter 1, we described David's first attempts to draw a train track after saying, "I can't draw." When his buddies, Tre and Jake, challenged him and demonstrated how to draw train tracks, he responded with a beautiful drawing and a proud smile to go with it.

This powerful experience led to others later in the year. David became much more of a risk taker, trying things that he might not have tried in the past. At the beginning of the year, David had a hard time choosing which snack plate to select. He needed help and encouragement for every decision. Beginning in November, David began to choose activities and plates for snack, and he began to ask others to play with him instead of waiting until someone approached him. He gained a confidence that continued to grow. In April, the child that had reported he couldn't draw produced beautiful pictures of sea turtles, jellyfish, and a killer whale. Again, Tre and Jake prompted him and encouraged him (Chapter 1). He had the confidence to try, and he succeeded, as Jake noted in his journal entry (Figure 2–1). He not only drew them with his buddies but drew them in class and at home. He presented a two-foot-long killer whale to Beth as a gift near the end of the year. He had most certainly gained the confidence to believe in himself as an artist.

During preparations for Earth Day, David stayed in Mary's class after all of the other preschoolers had returned to their own classroom. He wanted to help his group finish its papier-mâché globe (Chapter 1). When he was ready to go back to his classroom, Mary asked, "David, do you need someone to walk down to your room with you?"

"No, I can go myself," David said. "I am brave."

In one sentence, David summed up a year's worth of work and growth. He was brave. Most likely, he would have developed his bravery merely by maturing over the course of a school year, but we believe that the supportive and nurturing experience with his older buddies certainly furthered this process for David and for many of his peers as well.

For David and his buddies, the progress was gradual, gentle, and peaceful. The changes and adjustments were subtle and, for the most part, pleasant. Others experienced radically different relationships, due to personalities, determination, and personal agendas. The bravery required by other buddies each week took on another form. Some children became frustrated when their younger buddies behaved in uncooperative ways, when they hit or kicked or refused to listen during reading times. In order to protect the privacy of our students, we have chosen not to tell individual stories in this section, but we believe it is important to share the process of how we helped the children work through these social challenges.

In our school, we emphasize the importance of caring relationships and making a friendly, supportive place where all community members can reach out and connect to one another as residents of the community. We help children be more understanding of one another and more socially adept through the work we do.

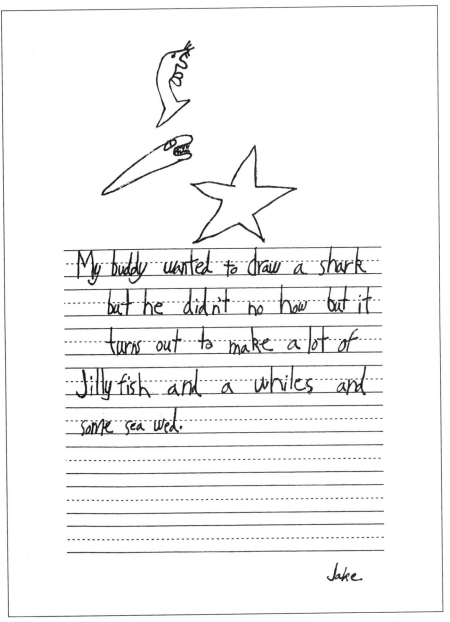

My buddy wanted to draw a shark
but he didn't no how but it
turns out to make a lot of
Jilly fish and a whiles and
some sea wed.

Jake

FIGURE 2–1 *Jake's Journal Entry*

We also believe it is important to help children solve problems themselves, rather than just passively follow adult directives. We work hard to help children think and develop a sense of being active agents of change. They learn that these changes don't occur overnight. As Merton (1961) writes, "Perfection is not something you can acquire like a hat—by walking into a place and trying on several and walking out again ten minutes later with one on your head that fits." Whatever we want to do well takes practice, and learning to be a successful buddy is no exception. This process happened primarily through our daily and weekly interactions and was refined through reflective conversations that followed each work session with the buddies. Preschoolers, appropriate to their age, usually did this by talking about buddy reading while choosing books to send to the older buddies, by discussing what would happen before they traveled to their buddies' classroom, and by communicating with the teacher following a buddy reading session when something seemed to be missing or a difficulty arose. Because of the mentor roles and relative maturity of the older children, much of the true reflective work occurred in the first- and second-grade class.

On a typical day, after paints were put away, floors were swept, and blocks were returned to their storage places, the first and second graders sat in a circle and Mary posed the question "How did it go today?" Hands flew in the air as many children requested the chance to share accomplishments, celebrate milestones, and seek assistance for problems that arose. This conversation was always entered into with a sense of respect for the community and any individuals whose names might be mentioned in the process. It was not a gossip session or a time to spread unkind words about someone; rather, it was a chance to improve the relationships that existed between our two classes.

We talked about the fact that even the best of buddies have their turbulent times and we all sometimes need help in getting to a place of being friendly and supportive. Stages of child development were often a topic of discussion. The children learned that all three- and four-year-olds—and even some six- and seven-year-olds—are in the process of learning appropriate social skills, appropriate ways to express anger, and appropriate negotiation skills. We talked about how young children often use their bodies to express themselves and need practice learning to wait, share, and work through disagreements.

If a specific problem arose and was identified, such as a buddy refusing to cooperate during an art project, talking during songs, or running away from the cooking table, Mary often asked another question: "How can we solve this problem?" The first and second graders, full of concern for their classmates as well as their buddies, were quick to produce solutions. These were offered verbally, or in some cases, written down in the form of a survey, and then voted on. Sample solutions on a given day might include the following:

- Stay calm.
- Keep your hands to yourself.
- Talk to your buddy.
- Don't use too much glue.
- Stay a role model.
- Ignore him.
- Use markers on paper only.

Talking Young Children Through Trying Times

When challenging situations arise, we find that children are more likely to be active problem solvers when they have a voice in determining the solutions. Here are some ideas we've used successfully in talking young children through problematic situations:

- *Talk honestly and openly about problems, emphasizing positive outcomes.*

- *Remind everyone to talk respectfully about others, whether they are present or not.*

- *Make sure the conversation is always moving toward the solution, rather than serving as a time to complain.*

- *Give children the language they need to articulate problems. For example, instead of saying, "He was mean to me," help the child describe a specific action, such as pinching, saying unkind words, or being distracted by something in the room.*

- *Help children move away from blaming others and see their own contributions to problematic situations.*

- *Remind everyone to report only direct experiences or observations rather than assumptions (e.g., "I heard her say this" versus "I think they were telling secrets").*

- *Always ask children to take the other's perspective, imagining how it felt to be in his or her position in the situation.*

- *Model being a good listener, a sincere advocate, and a compassionate friend.*

Always, the intent was to move forward with our buddies in a positive, productive manner.

Personal writing was a valuable means of problem solving and celebrating accomplishments for the older children. It often allowed them to have a perspective on situations that were on their minds and helped them develop a sense of personal responsibility. As is our practice in our everyday lives as learners, when we feel we have some ownership in helping solve problems, it empowers us to be more dedicated, more patient, and more accepting. Children respond in the same way. By including them in the process of coming up with solutions, either through conversation or through writing, we helped them remember what it was like to be three, and they helped their younger buddies move along the same socialization process they themselves had experienced.

The weekly logs Mary required the older buddies to keep for reflections on time spent with the younger class provided many examples and showed growth over time. In November, one child wrote the following:

> *When we were down at Beth's room I was cutting an apple. [My buddy] was talking to me. He was bothering me. So I accidentally cut my nail and it hurt. [He] was making a mess at his table. We did felt trains, apple peelings, and blocks. It was a lot of fun.*

Later in the school year, the same child wrote:

> *Today at buddy study my buddy behaved very well! Hooray!!! He even behaved when the fire drill went off. He also helped me make a mobile. It has seaweed with fish, more fish and star fish. It looks like a real mobile.*

Writing about buddies and their challenges appeared in other assignments. For Martin Luther King Jr. Day, the older students were asked to each think of one thing they do to keep Martin Luther King Jr.'s dream alive. They were asked to illustrate their ideas and write about them. One of the boys opted to write about his mission to help his buddy be a good citizen as his contribution to MLK's dream:

> *My buddy is bad sometimes, but he is also calm, but not a lot. I am glad he is my buddy reader, even though he is a little bit hard sometimes!! It is worth it.*

As the year progressed, other kinds of writing about buddies surfaced. Challenges turned into celebrations. This poem of appreciation was written by Julia, a first grader, about her relationship with her buddy:

THE SPECIAL PAIR

We walk together
love connecting and sinking
   into my skin
It floats in the air like a jumpy little
bird who is trying
   to catch a worm.
We walk in the warm sun like
little squirrels.
We're the special pair.
We love each other like magnets
that stick together.
We're the special pair.

FIGURE 2–2   *Brendon's Certificate for Sami*

End-of-year certificates were equally touching. Brendon's handmade certificate for Sami (Figure 2–2) was indicative of the love and care that grew as a result of the social learning experiences we shared.

As we look back on the growth of all the children and reflect on the social literacy that they acquired, we are reminded of something we have learned from Ralph Peterson. He writes: "In holistic education students are self-projects. Learning is personal. Others can help, but the learner has to do the work" (1992, 120). What our classes did together allowed each child to become a more successful self-project. The older children gained empathy for what teachers and parents experience as they attempt to guide young people in their lives in positive directions. Our shared work gave each child the tools and confidence to move forward as a social being, better equipped to do the important life work that is presented to us each and every day.

Three

All Aboard: Community Literacy

Mary's class is aflutter with excitement. The butterfly larvae have just arrived to use with the kit they received as a thank-you gift for participating in a demonstration lesson at the local university. The caterpillars' arrival will turn the big cardboard box and a bunch of cups full of hungry larvae into a beautiful butterfly garden. Sean takes on the responsibility of setting up the kit and we decide he should take it (with Mona, the classroom assistant) to Beth's class because they are experts at butterflies, having just hatched their own batch of butterflies. The kit indicates there are twenty-five caterpillars inside, just slightly more than the number of students in Mary's class. Along with the cups and caterpillars comes enough food to last them through their larval stage. Sean and Mona scoop up food and caterpillars for each class member. When they are done, Sean counts the number of caterpillars. In the split second between counting caterpillars and students in his class, he has a realization. He calls out to Beth, "Hey, there are twelve caterpillars left. Do you think your kids might want them?" Beth asks him to run down and make sure it is okay with Mary and the rest of the buddies. It is, of course.

The preschoolers are excited and grateful that their buddies want to share such a wonderful experience with them. They immediately name their caterpillars—after themselves, their dogs, favorite characters, or friends. Every day, the children watch for signs that their caterpillars are transforming. On the day we see fine webs forming and caterpillars half covered, we carefully place them in the butterfly

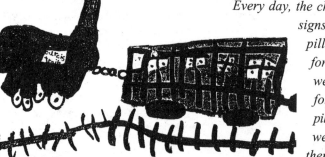

garden in Mary's classroom. When the butterflies begin to emerge, Mary's students report the news to their buddies with great excitement. We plan a special day to release the butterflies.

The day of the event comes. At first there is a frenzy to hold and release a butterfly. The older children crowd around to get their chance first. About five minutes into the releasing ceremony, the older children realize that their young buddies are not participating. Soon Anna passes the butterfly on her finger to Sami, Andrew shares his with Michael, and Sean finds a butterfly left in the box to share with Clara. As we watch the butterflies depart for their lives in the big world, we can't help but think that our daily work with these children is preparing them for the day that they, too, will fly off to new places. The community we have created together will make their wings strong and steady as they find their way.

As we observed the children in our classrooms working on aspects of their social growth, we realized something larger seemed to be occurring. Our experience and history, joint celebrations and rituals, play, and caring born of work together created a strong sense of community between our classrooms. We were compelled to work together as teachers and as classes by the community feeling between us as individuals and as a larger entity. We continued working together because these bonds became stronger and we all benefited from our collaborative time. An interesting aspect of the arrangement involved the physical setup of our classrooms. The rooms were physically as far apart as any classes could be in our school. This fact became irrelevant. We were so tied as a community that the distance didn't make a difference. Hearts bridged the distance. The students would walk down the hall to see their buddies, steal moments to chat and be with them whenever possible, and become excited whenever the opportunity presented itself to do a favor for the teacher that included visiting their buddies' classroom.

The flexibility of the school was also an integral factor in the success of our buddy community. The spirit of adventure and exploration found throughout the school allowed us to try new things. Others not directly involved in our buddy study were eager to lend suggestions and advice. One teacher, during the preparations for the winter solstice program, suggested that our two classes might want to perform together because it was Beth's first year and because there seemed to be a strong collaborative spirit between the two classes. It was obvious to many that we were a community that operated more like an extended family.

It's All Relative
_____

Ralph Peterson (1992) writes:

> *One could use the word* family *to describe life in a learning community, since the same underlying structures that appear in a healthy family*

occur in the classroom. Not many parents keep their children still and quiet all day long. They encourage their children to be expressive, to collaborate, to take risks, and to learn from failure by reflecting on what has happened. Isn't it only common sense for teachers to put the same principles to use in school? (3)

The reading buddies and teachers made up a new classroom family with unique ties to one another. A few children were going through difficult situations outside of school. In several cases, the buddies' teacher became a friend (like an aunt who is close) who could be someone to talk to and bond with who wasn't their teacher or parent. This gave them the opportunity to have a relationship with a trust-worthy adult who was not immediately involved in the situation or in a position of authority and who could also be a supportive listener. The sense of family made comfortable outside adult relationships possible.

Several students were from families in which they were the only child. The buddy environment provided unique opportunities for these children to practice socialization skills they didn't have a chance to practice in their homes with siblings. The structure closely resembled a family situation, which included sibling rivalry, vying for the "parents'" attention, as well as the closeness families have during both joyful and sad times. For example, when Ruby, an elephant at the Phoenix Zoo, died, many of the children grieved deeply for her. She had been a favorite of theirs as far back as they could remember and they were struggling with their feelings about her death. One of the things for which Ruby was famous was her paintings. Occasionally she was given a canvas and a paintbrush and she would paint colorful splashes on the white space. The paintings were later sold as a fund-raiser for the zoo. Tati and Theo's family owned one of Ruby's paintings and the day they brought it to share with all of the buddies helped many of the children deal with the sadness they felt about Ruby's death.

Like siblings, sometimes children would argue to see who would run a note down the hallway to Mary or Beth. On other occasions, the same children could be observed offering comfort and friendship to a classmate who was feeling sad or left out. The sense of family enabled the children to experience a wide range of responses to real-life situations. They received guidance and felt secure, knowing they could expand their social skills in a safe community.

Two other factors that allowed us to do what we did with the children were the willingness and support we got from our other "family members," Mona and Renee, our classroom aides. They accepted the processes and often crazy ideas that the teachers and students had. There were many activities that were rather labor-intensive for the teachers and aides. Cookie-making days (Figure 3–1) demanded making dough with the children, a messy process that tried everyone's patience; keeping a good flour supply on the table to avoid stickiness; and providing lots

Benefits of a Close-Knit School Community

- *You don't have to go visit your relatives very often because you feel like you spend every weekday with cousins, aunts, and uncles.*

- *There is a strong sense of belonging to a group that shares common interests, values, and priorities.*

- *Teachers, school staff, parents, and children develop a history over time, which allows for more of a "village" approach to child rearing.*

- *The level of caring is deeper, and each teacher continues relationships with families long after a child has been in his or her classroom.*

- *The possibilities for problem solving increase because more people have a vested interest in situations that arise.*

- *Children have opportunities to establish sibling-like relationships over many years with other children of different ages, which strengthens their sense of belonging to the greater world community.*

Tips for Cookie Makers

If you were brave enough to try papier-mâché, how about giving cookies a whirl?

- *Wear comfortable, washable clothing—you will get messy.*

- *Try your dough recipe first to make sure it isn't too sticky or too difficult to work with.*

- *Make sure you have TONS of sprinkles to avoid a sprinkle shortage crisis.*

- *Have lots of help around that day for assistance and cleanup.*

- *Make sure to coat the table with flour and have plenty of it handy to keep dough from sticking to the table.*

- *Make the dough as a math project.*

- *Make sure your oven is really tall, so the mounds of sprinkles won't burn from touching the heating unit.*

FIGURE 3–1 *Cookie Making*

and lots of assistance with the cutouts, decorations, and, again, intensive cleanup. Mona and Renee simply smiled and jumped right in, with occasional and minimal coaxing. Their willingness to support our spontaneous ideas gave us the extra energy we needed to keep our community of buddies thriving with new possibilities.

With Real Life in Mind

One important aspect of our community was the purposefulness of our time together. The students made lists and brainstormed ideas for what to do, or we planned activities around the interests and ideas of the children. The ideas of the children often involved family-like activities. At the end of the year, when we brainstormed one final time to see what the kids wanted to do, the ideas included baking or cooking, sharing meals, dressing up, playing with cars, water play, and so on (see list in Chapter 1). In fact, when reviewing favorite activities for the year, most students listed these things as their most-loved buddy experiences of the year.

A Shared History

Community was also built upon a sense of history. As our students met weekly at first and more frequently later on, our shared common background grew. Near the end of the school year, the students fondly remembered the year and the many experiences we shared. When the first and second graders listed the accomplishments of which they were most proud, their preschool buddies were often mentioned.

The shared history developed as a result of many occurrences, some planned and others more spontaneous. We noticed some general influences that contributed to it. They were

- regular routines and rituals
- celebrations
- honoring and appreciation
- a sense of responsibility

Building on Everyday Matters: Routines and Rituals

Learning to be a literate community member, like other literacies, takes practice. Much of that practice occurs through daily and weekly routines and rituals. The predictable and repetitive routines of choosing books, delivering them to the other class, and then collecting them at the end of buddy reading each week allowed our students to move about their daily school lives with a sense of order and ownership. Reading with a buddy, followed by sharing a story with both classes together became more than a routine, however. These weekly activities functioned as rituals, which transported our community to a different reality where we operated on the feeling level, rather than doing activities guided by reason (Peterson 1992).

Singing together was one of our most powerful rituals. It was one of the first things we found we could do together that bridged the age gap between classes. We met on equal terms during singing. It drew the children in, focused their attention, and calmed them down in preparation for the day's work. Our singing ritual transformed us as well. As we taught one another songs, and worked at learning with and from one another, a mutual enjoyment of the process occurred. Our collective body of shared knowledge, acquired via the songs we learned, was something in which our community took great pride. There was excitement when a new song was added to the collection, especially in the case of new train songs.

Routines and Rituals—Not Just Time Management

- *Imagine all the routines and rituals that your family has. They bind individuals together, creating community and a sense of belonging.*
- *Routines help us manage the ordinary parts of the school day, freeing up time for extraordinary things to happen.*
- *Singing, dancing, and drama seem to be particularly good for creating acceptance and group cohesion.*
- *If children help create the ritual, performing it helps solidify the group as having similar belief systems, wishes, and needs.*
- *Ritual helps us renew our commitment to that in which we believe.*
- *When we perform rituals, we allow ourselves to open our minds for creativity, for deeper thought, and for meaningful discussion.*

During one buddy session, we spent our entire time singing, savoring a celebration of song, our relationships, and being human.

Breaking Bread: Celebrations

A natural extension of our experience together was sharing meals and celebrations. During our Thanksgiving celebration mentioned in Chapter 1, the younger children sat interspersed with the older children and chatted away as if they were members of a huge family gathered for a holiday meal. There was such a strong sense of community among the children that we adults found ourselves with no place to sit at the table. We all thought this was quite entertaining and enjoyed the fact that our classes were so self-contained that they didn't need us to supervise or keep order.

Valentine's Day brought the aforementioned cookie project. The classes decided that the best way to celebrate would be to make cookies and eat them on Valentine's Day. The classes rolled out the dough, cut it with cookie cutters, and placed it on waiting cookie sheets, where the cookies were decorated and made ready for baking. They looked more like mounds of sprinkles with a little dough underneath than cookies (Figure 3–2). We baked them during recess and shared them later on that morning. Buddies exchanged special valentines they had made for one another secretly in their individual classes. The older buddies even wrote

FIGURE 3–2   *Sprinkles*

love poems for their special little friends (Figure 3–3). We watched and shared our own valentines on this special day to remember.

Mother's Day preparations mentioned in Chapter 1 were remarkable days for our classes as well for building community. The shared art and writing experience in honor of mothers was meaningful and fun, but it also connected us in another way. We realized as the process evolved that we all had the common experience of having a mother. The conversations that occurred and comments about why we love our mothers elevated the experience for all of us. Statements about mothers, such as three-year-old Betty's "I love my mommy because she gives me ice cream," triggered off a series of stories and memories involving mothers. It was just one more way in which we found we were tied as a community.

Later in the year, there seemed to be more and more assumptions that we would do things together. After a spring fund-raiser, our parents organization donated some of the proceeds for an end-of-year pizza party. It was a celebration in honor of the hard work all of the children did to raise money for a new climbing structure for our school. When we discussed the idea with our classes, they decided, not surprisingly, that we should have the pizza party together. The children laughed and ate pizza in celebration of a job well done.

FIGURE 3–3 *Tre's Poem for David*

One of our best celebrations was at the end of the semester, when we had a going away party for Aimee, Mary's student teacher. She was dear to all of us. The students gathered in Beth's class, where secret preparations could occur without Aimee knowing. The preschoolers carefully painted a huge heart for her to show her how they felt. The students in Mary's class made beautiful self-portraits out of cut paper, which they then put together and framed to make a paper quilt. The children gave their beautiful artwork to her before we sang songs in celebration. We asked Aimee to choose the songs. Afterward, all the students gathered on the playground just outside Beth's room to share a favorite frozen treat, popsicles.

Michael, then four, walked up to Mary in great camaraderie and said, "Hey, Mary, we match." Beth looked Mary and Michael up and down in confusion. Mary and Beth, dumbfounded, continued to search for signs of matching. Mary had a grape popsicle, Michael had a cherry one. What could it be? Beth finally asked, "How do you match, Michael?" Michael cheerfully said, "We have the same *stick!*" and walked away, pleased at his connection with Mary. The statement was an end to a great celebration and a statement about our strong community bonding!

For Those Who Care: Honoring and Appreciation

The *Rule of St. Benedict* (Fry 1982), a guide for monastic communities, states that all guests should be welcomed, treated with kindness, and addressed with humility upon arrival or departure. Although we were far from a monastic community, making others feel at ease and accepted was an important aspect of our collective community. Acknowledging difficulties, offering wishes for healing, and showing appreciation for something special were all ways we accomplished this. For example, when three-year-old Tori was sick, the buddies made a poster that everyone signed to send her get-well wishes. When Beth became ill, an immediate request from one of Mary's students was for time to make her a card. Thank-you notes traveled back and forth between classes, and those who made significant contributions to our community were earnestly acknowledged. One of the most notable cards was a large green piece of cardboard that the preschoolers sent to their buddies during the December holidays. It had gingerbread train cars with loads of glitter on them.

Thank-You Card Bonus Idea

If you have a cooking project that goes awry (e.g., cup of salt is added instead of a cup of sugar, or the cookies get baked for twenty minutes instead of the recommended ten), think twice before tossing those cookies! Instead, find a big piece of cardboard, paint it a bright color, and glue the inedible cookies on. Sprinkle some glitter on for accent, write your message, and you have a giant thank-you card from one class to another.

Warning: *Sitting underneath such a card hung on the wall could be hazardous to one's head. Make sure the cookies are glued on really well, or they might fall off.*

Math idea: *If one of the cookies looks like it is going to fall off, estimate how long it will take for it to hit the floor.*

Our celebration for Aimee when she finished her student teaching was another excellent example of this kind of honoring.

Acknowledgments of community membership were not limited to teachers. When four-year-old Marcel moved, his preschool classmates and older buddies alike were heartbroken. After his last day, the classes decided to make a special book so that Marcel would have something by which to remember them. They put together a book of memories and even bits of advice for him. First grader Anna wrote:

> *Dear Marcel,*
>
> *I think you will have a good new school. But if you want to visit us you can. If you be nice to people in the future they'll be nice to you too. That was just a tip. We'll miss you. Hope you visit soon! From, Anna*

One of the most touching moments of appreciation was after Beth's class held the sale to raise money to adopt the whale. Her children decided that they should do something special for their buddies. They assisted Renee in making fresh batches of Rice Crispy Treats and Chex Mix, which had both been sale favorites. The small children, used to creating spectacular thank-you cards for many individuals by then, decided to paint a picture that would show their big buddies their gratitude. The preschoolers presented their gifts to the buddies in a heartwarming gesture the next Tuesday morning during buddy project time. Furthermore, Mary's class, which had eagerly helped out with the sale just for the sake of being helpful, was surprised and grateful when a whale adoption certificate arrived with "Mary's Class" written on it, along with the one for Beth's class. These acts of kindness and appreciation were quiet gestures that spoke loudly of the value we all placed on our community.

Another kind of appreciation occurred between classes when something remarkable happened in one or the other. Early in the year, the preschoolers made a sleeping bag for a homeless boy. They worked hard pasting material on quilt squares, learning how a sewing machine works, helping a student's mother sew the squares together, and assisting in the strategic placement of the ties that held the front, batting, and back together. They were very proud of their efforts. When it was done, the first thing the young children did was ask to bring the sleeping bag to the buddies' classroom to show their workmanship. The older children were impressed and helped the younger ones see what a wonderful job they had done. Self-esteem was built and ties were made through this experience.

Later in the year, after Beth and her friend Martin had spent weeks building, staining, and assembling a large loft for her classroom, the excited loft owners asked Beth if their buddies could be the first other class to see it. Beth said, "Yes, of course." Everyone proudly took a turn climbing the ladder and inspecting the

> ## *Appreciation Gift Possibilities*
>
> - *baked treats*
> - *handmade cards (individual or from the whole group)*
> - *class quilt (do individual collages on squares of paper and put them together like a quilt, or use cloth with fabric crayons or photo transfers if you have a longer work period)*
> - *posters (use watercolor or tempera paint; handprints add a nice touch)*
> - *collection of poems or pictures*
> - *potted plants grown from seeds*
> - *magnetic picture frames made with popsicle sticks and found objects*
> - *individual poems (e.g., for Valentine's Day)*
> - *pasta necklaces (dyed with food coloring so you can make patterns)*
> - *book with a collection of letters*

well-crafted loft, which became a favorite reading spot for our community for the remainder of the year.

Responsibility

Rituals we shared, our sense of family, and celebrations and other assorted activities we did to show appreciation for one another all played a role in the development of community literacy. Along with these, an awareness of the importance of responsibility also grew. Our students learned that for our community of buddies to thrive, we needed to look out for one another. This was particularly true for the older children with their young buddies. In the mornings on the playground before school, a few of the preschoolers sometimes became distressed when their parents left for the day. It was common to see the older child run over to the gate, stand by her waving—and sometimes tearful—little buddy, and immediately try to distract him or engage him in an activity that would remove the departing parent from his mind. After school, when the preschoolers were in the process of waking up from their naps, older buddies frequently offered support, back rubs, or simply someone to talk to until they were fully awake.

The older children were available and excited to help at other times, too. Sean, age eight, said to Beth, "I love the little kids. Can I please come to your classroom and help?"

During the winter solstice practice and performance, this sense of responsibility was most obvious. The older children helped their buddies know where to go and what to do. The younger ones, in turn, demonstrated their responsibility to the community by following directions, listening, and responding according to the plan. At the end of the program, a parent from another class commented, "It is obvious that these children knew each other well by the way they performed together."

Responsibility to the community took on other forms as well. When Beth's class first proposed the idea for the sale, the older children's immediate reaction was "What are we going to do to help?" The community became so strong that almost everything of significance to one class automatically became a joint project.

Dance Rehearsals or World Federation Wrestling? You Be the Judge . . .

- *If, in a moment of insanity, you decide you want to try choreographing a dance to be performed by a group of thirty-four students ranging in ages from three to eight, pause and think again.*
- *If you still think it's a good idea, provide mats for the dancers wrestling on the sidelines while others are practicing.*
- *Pick the music first. It will give you a foundation upon which to build the dance.*
- *Use the children's ideas for movement. Have them dance around freely and use their movements for parts of the dance.*
- *Give a name to each movement as you add it to your dance (e.g., Susanna's spin-hop, Mike's airplane lunge).*
- *Work on smaller parts and then add on. Bring in the younger children after the older ones have the first part established.*
- *Have faith that even though every practice might be a nightmare, the children will actually pull through for the performance.*

All Aboard: Community Literacy

58

The strength of the community created an important sense of belonging. If a buddy was missing on a Friday, the children automatically and aggressively pursued a working arrangement that would give everyone a buddy and help everyone feel he or she belonged. It got to the point where we didn't have to be involved in this pairing-up process at all; the children took responsibility for it. As the children became more literate in the ways of being community members, they were able to move away from merely thinking about their personal needs and take on the perspectives of others. As this process occurred, there was a growing awareness that the needs of others were important, not just in our small community of buddies, but in a more global sense. Something deeper than just being a good citizen in our immediate situation began to come forth. Through what we did on a daily basis with one another, we started seeing how our lives and the lives of others might be influenced in a broader way. We caught glimpses of a new generation of humanitarians about to burst forth into the world.

Four

Toward a Landscape of Kindness: Humanitarian Literacy

Eight-year-old Kelsey sits down at the art table, preparing to make her holiday gift for her three-year-old buddy, Travis, who has autism. It is mid-December and a flurry of activity fills the entire school. Amidst the rehearsals for our winter solstice performance, last-minute touches on the poetry collection for parents, and holiday visits to the nursing home, the first and second graders are making ornaments for their buddies. Kelsey gathers the materials she needs: popsicle sticks, glitter, glue, scrap paper, yarn, and scissors. As she settles in her chair, she looks up at Mary with her sparkling, brown eyes and says with heartfelt sincerity, "I'm making a star for Travis so he can get better from his disease."

Kelsey's comment summarized in the deepest way what our buddy study was all about. She made Travis a gift for the holiday season; it was something she did as a friend and community member, knowing through our studies what a challenging road he faces. In addition to all of the other literacies we've mentioned, her words confirmed another level of literacy emergent in our collaboration, that of learning to be a better human being. Kelsey's comment was somewhat of an epiphany for us as we continued our examination of the many dimensions of the relationships between our two classes and the community we had become.

What we noticed with the children was a level of caring that went beyond just being friendly or kind to their buddies. Something extraordinary occurred, and we saw it in many aspects of our daily classroom lives. It was recognized by parents as well. What we noticed were emerging patterns that not only helped the children be good friends in their immediate situation but also produced the potential for lifelong implications. As we watched Kelsey and Melisa patiently help Travis build a tower with blocks over and over, it made us wonder to what extent this experience might influence their future career choices, their interactions with others who are different in some way, and their ability to show leadership in situations where empathy is required. For other children, too, such as Deana, who thoughtfully demonstrated to her little buddy, Caitlin, how to be a successful reader (Figure 4–1), and Jake, who taught David how to draw sharks, this experience seemed to hold much more than the immediate encounter. All of the children—and their teachers—carried something away from the year that we believe will influence the rest of their lives, consciously or in more subtle ways. Their process of becoming more literate humanitarians taught them these primary lessons:

- It takes practice to become a better human being.
- By celebrating differences, our lives are enriched.
- Being a kind and compassionate person matters.
- Mindfulness in how we treat others changes lives, including our own.
- Mentoring helps us grow as learners and leaders.
- When we help others through service, we also help ourselves.

FIGURE 4–1 *Deana and Caitlin Reading*

Transporting the Bags

Early in the year, Sami brought in the sturdy canvas bags to use any way we wished. Each bag had a zipper and a little pocket for inserting a name card. It didn't take long to figure out how to use them; they were perfect for the weekly buddy book selections. The older buddies picked out books from their class and the preschoolers made their choices as well, usually early in the week, and put them in the bags. The bags were placed in a big blue basket and carried to the other end of the long hallway to Mary's class, so the first and second graders could practice them for buddy reading on Friday. The process of delivering and returning the books was an important and desired activity for many children, and it became somewhat of a practice in itself. As the year progressed, when anything needed to be transported from either room to the other, there was always a crowd of volun-

---

Everyday Ways to Promote Kindness

- *Make cards at every opportunity to say "sorry you are sick," "thank you," "congratulations," or anything else you can think of.*

- *Have children (even preschoolers) begin to think of ways to do things for others. When presented with a situation or problem, they will often do this themselves. For example, three-year-olds wanted to make blankets for children who were homeless because everyone needs a blanket, and they wanted to donate items to those who lost their home to a tornado that year.*

- *Suggest, once or twice, that if you're doing something for yourselves, you also do it for another class. We often cook enough snacks for our friends' classes and share with them. Soon, the children will suggest it.*

- *Send notes to buddies and create art for them.*

- *Model the behavior yourself; this is the best way for them to learn.*

- *Point out examples of things others have done. Celebrate when someone is spontaneously kind.*

- *Encourage empathy. Problem solve with children about how to help another child in distress.*

teers eager to fulfill the duty. The delivery system became more sophisticated as the practice of sending and receiving evolved. For example, when a large, heavy container of seashells needed to be returned to Mary, a few of Beth's students completed the job by pushing the container down the hall on a chair with wheels. When Beth's class was studying artist Jackson Pollock, Tori and Sami were sent to Mary's class to find examples of his work in some of Mary's art books. When the suitable book—a large, heavy volume—was found, Sami and Tori prepared to lug it back to their room. Susanna, a perceptive second grader, noticed this and offered, "I better help them carry it to their room—it's really heavy."

Just as the children became more accomplished at fulfilling their errand duties and learned to be more engaging readers and attentive listeners with one another, they also worked on being better citizens. Words like *kindness, patience,* and *respect* were everyday words in our classrooms. The application of them was another story, and it took practice. Our daily lives together provided many opportunities. Kelsey and Melisa, with their buddy, Travis, provided a significant example.

Secure With *The Cat in the Hat*

We assigned the buddies the first week of school, mostly taking a guess at the pairings. We were fairly certain of one thing—that Travis would need just the right buddies. Diagnosed with autism a few months prior to his enrollment in our school, Travis was accompanied by a therapist who assisted him in his daily routine. We knew he loved books and we wanted to draw on that strength and interest. After careful consideration, we selected two friends, Kelsey and Melisa, to be his buddies. We chose Kelsey because she has an energetic, determined personality and Melisa because of her experience with a younger brother and her empathy for others. They were a perfect team.

Kelsey and Melisa discovered that Travis loved Dr. Seuss and included many of his books in their earliest buddy reading sessions. On buddy reading day, they sat in a tight cluster on the floor, the two girls taking turns reading as Travis sat on his therapist's lap, completely engrossed in the story. Getting him to listen to books was easy; enticing him to do other activities and listen to other books besides *The Cat in the Hat* took more skillful means. Coached by Travis' teachers, they learned numerous techniques for getting Travis to respond. For example, when they wanted him to add his contribution to the ABC train book, they showed him how to cut small pieces of paper with scissors and then said, "Travis, do this." When he became distracted by something else, they waited for him to make eye contact and then repeated their request. When we learned about him using Dr. Seuss as an escape, his buddies worked hard to focus his attention away from Dr. Seuss books and use them as a reward for listening to other titles. They even went so far as to hide the whole collection of Dr. Seuss books they'd carefully assembled because they knew it would be a distraction.

Kelsey and Melisa were supported in their work with Travis. A few weeks into the school year, a specialist came to talk to both classes about autism. The preschoolers did a study of autism in class, as did the first and second graders, who came up with this list of information they learned:

- Don't laugh at people with autism if they do funny things like sniff bricks.
- Help them do things that are difficult, like if they can't understand or communicate.
- If a person with autism is about to do something dangerous, get help. Don't let them climb high places. Don't let them out of your sight.
- Sing a song with them if they have trouble waiting in line.
- People with autism think a little bit differently than most people.
- Sometimes people with autism do dangerous things because they get mixed-up ideas from movies, video games, and books or TV shows. They get confused between what's real and what's not.
- Try to do sign language with them.
- People with autism might feel like they're in their own world.
- Don't use an excited voice when you talk to someone with autism. Talk slowly and clearly.
- If they get too active, read them a book.

It didn't take long for many of the children to begin applying what they learned from the specialist and from the class study. One thing the specialist mentioned was the importance of including children with autism in as many ways as possible. A few days later, both classes happened to be on the playground for recess at the same time. We looked over at the sand area and noticed Kelsey, Melisa, and a few friends playing ring-around-the-rosy, with Travis as an active participant. This went on for about fifteen minutes, and later, when the group dispersed, we observed the girls using sign language with him. Including Travis became their yearlong mission.

The situation with Travis went beyond trying to be helpful or tolerating someone who is different. They genuinely wanted to take a proactive part in facilitating his learning process, as was demonstrated by their playground game, and they somehow knew that their acts of kindness would make a difference in his life.

Budding Humanitarians

The experience of including and learning to understand a child with differences was exemplified by Kelsey and Melisa's relationship with Travis. Their work with him and his joyful response to their caring affected all of us. What occurred with the buddies, however, was more encompassing than embracing and including differences. What we all learned was that kindness and compassion matter; in fact, there is little that matters more. As the Dalai Lama said, "Love and compassion are necessities, not luxuries. Without them, humanity cannot survive" (Brussat and Brussat 1996, 325).

Peaceful Heroes

- *Mahatma Gandhi*
- *Rosa Parks*
- *Ruby Bridges*
- *Martin Luther King Jr.*
- *H. H. the Dalai Lama*
- *George Washington Carver*
- *Susan B. Anthony*
- *Elizabeth Cady Stanton*
- *H. H. the Karmapa*
- *Joan Baez*
- *Fannie Lou Hamer*
- *Jackie Robinson*
- *Pete Seeger*
- *Bob Dylan*
- *Mother Teresa*
- *Cathy Freeman*
- *Woody Guthrie*
- *Peter, Paul, and Mary*
- *Aung San Suu Kyi*
- *Thich Nhat Hanh*
- *Thomas Merton*

Within many spiritual traditions, there are men and women who are considered fully realized or awakened beings. Mother Teresa, Mahatma Gandhi, and the Dalai Lama are but a few. In the Tibetan tradition, they are known as bodhisattvas. "A Bodhisattva is someone with pure, impeccable intentions—a gentle yet fearless spiritual warrior who strives unceasingly to help everyone reach . . . peace and enlightenment" (Das 1997, 143). These spiritual seekers will make a commitment to living a life of kindness until each and every living creature also knows that same kindness. We tried to model this for our students and support them in their efforts to interact with one another in kind ways. It was part of their social literacy, but it also went deeper. Through our work together, we helped them see that how they treated one another would not only affect their immediate situation but would also lay a foundation for the kind of people they would become. We spent considerable time in both classes talking about the importance of empathy and compassion for others. We discussed the fact that when we are kind to others, kindness will be shown in return. In *Tuesdays with Morrie* (Albom 1997), this idea is well-expressed: "Do the kinds of things that come from the heart. When you do, you won't be dissatisfied, you won't be envious, you won't be longing for somebody else's trip. On the contrary, you'll be overwhelmed with what comes back" (128). When our classes were together, we tried to do things from the heart, and this was at no time more evident than the day we went to the nursing home.

Mary's class made biweekly visits to a local nursing home throughout the school year. Every other Monday morning, the students boarded the care center's van to spend an hour and a half singing, working on art projects, celebrating special occasions, and exchanging stories with the residents. It was a gratifying experience for everyone because we knew we were helping their lives to be more meaningful and happy. Furthermore, it brought out the best in the children, knowing their kindness mattered to the residents. As the year progressed, we thought it might be interesting to include the preschool buddies in one of the nursing home visits. In late April it finally happened.

Prior to the visit, Beth prepared her students for what they would likely experience. The preschoolers read books about the elderly, watched a video to help them understand what they might encounter, and discussed why people are in nursing homes. It was Beth's feeling that they should be well-informed so they would be unafraid of what they might see. She reassured them that familiar adults would be there if they needed help. Soon they all reported their readiness and excitement for the trip.

On the day of the visit, we all arrived, ready to make spring flowers among friends young and old. The older children, already comfortable in the nursing home setting, were conscientious about making their buddies feel at ease. They helped them get set up at a table near a resident to work on the day's project. Each found a place of comfort, some on the laps of residents, most in chairs beside their new elder friends in their wheelchairs. Shy David, with his mother's encouragement, was one of the first to find a nursing home friend, and with his buddy, he produced enough flowers for several residents.

Why an Intergenerational Program?

- *Everybody wins: elders have regular contact with the youthful energy of children, and children gain experience with the joys and challenges of the aging process.*
- *It gives children an opportunity to be compassionate and patient in new ways unlike those available in everyday school settings.*
- *It provides elders something to look forward to and gives them hope and encouragement.*
- *It helps children appreciate their good health and energy.*
- *It enables some elders to remember their childhood memories and tell stories.*
- *It gives children experience with death and the dying process with someone they care about, but who isn't immediate family.*
- *It allows children a chance to see that elders have lives, histories, and feelings, too.*
- *It helps create a greater sense of connectedness to the life cycle and each person's place in it.*

Several of David's classmates proved themselves to be delightful visitors as well. One child, who first thought he'd rather leave the room than join in the activities with the residents, settled in nicely after a reassuring hug from Beth. He ended up remaining at the table, smiling, talking happily, giving hugs, and creating some of the most innovative paper flowers of the day. Another three-year-old responded so well to the residents that she began singing. Soon the resident nearby was singing along, each doing a verse and joining in on the chorus together.

As we departed from the nursing home that day, there was a mixture of feelings. Everyone was excited for having completed a successful outing together with our buddies. A sense of pride filled the air as older buddies held the hands of their younger friends, who adjusted comfortably to a new environment and did everything they were supposed to do. But more than anything, in different ways we all seemed to leave knowing that the kindness and compassion we showed to the residents mattered to them and, even if for a short time, made their day a little brighter.

Ever Mindful

In the beginning of the year, it was the responsibility of the older buddies to select books to read on Fridays. As the younger children grew more accustomed to the school routine, they were given the opportunity to select books as well, to fill up their green canvas bags. At first they chose books that were personally interesting, often picking the same books three weeks in a row. When Beth encouraged them to expand their selections beyond their favorites, they chose books that had topics they liked or they thought their buddies might like. When one child noticed a book about snakes, he suggested Sami take it to her buddy because he knew Brendon was interested in snakes. One of the most significant selections came one day in February when almost-four-year-old Antonio was searching for the right books for one of his buddies. Aware that his older buddy was still an emerging reader at the time, he said, "I'm looking for one that's not so long, not a lot of words." He knew what his buddy needed to be a successful reader because he had paid attention.

Part of our work as buddies included developing an awareness of others and their needs. Antonio's careful book selection was a good example of this. It was certainly tied in with practicing kindness and compassion, but it was also slightly separate in that it was a way we learned to be more observant, more mindful of what we were doing.

> *When we talk about mindfulness, we are describing conscious living and alert presence of mind. Mindfulness helps us bring our innate awareness into sharper focus; it helps us pay attention to what we are doing as we are doing it. Paying attention helps us live in, and appreciate, the present moment in all its richness and depth. It helps us see—truly see—what is actually going on. Simply put, paying attention pays off. (Das 1999, 190)*

When Antonio said he wanted to find a book with easier text, it was an indication that he not only listened to the stories his buddies had been reading to him for several months but also paid attention to their process as readers. His awareness of what his buddy needed and his request for a book to support his growth as a reader helped everyone involved be more successful—as a reader, as a person, and as a friend. Because he had paid attention, Antonio's request also became an act of thoughtfulness.

Learning to be mindful was an ongoing process in both of our classrooms. It was emphasized when we talked about social interactions and relationships, but it also spilled over into other aspects of our lives together. Mindfulness was a part of discussions about picking up trash from the playground and included in responses to the needs of others, near and far. When Beth's class discussed the tor-

> ### *How to Encourage Mindfulness in Children*
> - *Catch children when the moment is ripe for learning—just before something is going to happen. Have them reflect on the situation and make good choices.*
> - *Stop during the day to imagine something happening with the children and ask them how they would handle it.*
> - *Role-play any chance you get.*
> - *Ask frequently when things come up in class, "What would the best decision be in this situation?"*
> - *Stop the daily action to acknowledge and celebrate acts of mindfulness.*

nadoes that had devastated Oklahoma residents, one of her students responded with a request to do something to help "the tomato victims." They made the sleeping bag for a homeless boy without a "blankie," mentioned in Chapter 3. The more we paid attention and developed mindfulness, the more able we were to respond in thoughtful, considerate ways. In doing so, we learned to "see with receptive eyes and discover a world of ceaseless wonders" (Brussat and Brussat 1996, 19). As the children in our classes took notice of what needed care and attention in their immediate surroundings, they began to understand the meaning of service. They learned that through service they could make a difference in the world, for others and for themselves.

May I Help You, Please?

As we mentioned earlier in the book, when the preschoolers decided they wanted to have a sale to raise money to adopt the whale, the older children immediately jumped on the project also. In part, this was due to the close-knit community that formed between the two classes over the course of the year. Additionally, it seemed like a fun project to be involved with that would make use of everyone's creative talents. But there was also something deeper at work. Brussat and Brussat (1996) write, "There is deep satisfaction to be gained in working together with others on service projects. It is one of the best ways to diminish the power of fear, helplessness, and hopelessness (326)." When the buddies worked together on the sale, it gave them all a sense of doing something; something that would make a difference in the world. Doing it collaboratively only strengthened that commitment and sense of empowerment. According to Kirby (1989), "Service brings together students from diverse ethnic and socioeconomic groups. It enables students to give something back to their schools and communities. It creates positive partnerships between students and adults by encouraging youth to make the transition to adulthood as contributing and caring members of society. Finally, it encourages a lifelong commitment to the service ethic." Through the project, they felt that what they were doing was important and would improve the condition of life for another creature on the planet.

Community Service Projects for Children

- *Work for Project Linus, an organization that provides blankets for children.*
- *Join local canned food drives.*
- *Adopt an animal. Be careful how you explain this to very young children; one child expected to bring a whale we were adopting into our classroom because when she was adopted, she came to live with her new family.*
- *Send packages of supplies and needed items to disaster victims. (Contact the American Red Cross.)*
- *Visit and bring needed items to nursing homes.*
- *Collect items for transitional centers for victims of domestic violence.*
- *In school,*
  - *Clean up the playground.*
  - *Help another class with work it is doing.*
  - *Offer services to administration or janitors.*
  - *Plant flowers.*

Involvement in a service project such as the whale adoption fund-raiser, visiting elderly residents in a nursing home, or even something as mundane as helping return materials from one class to another helps set the stage for a life of service to others. Learning the value of service at a young age not only improves a child's self-esteem but establishes a foundation for being a good citizen with vision to see how we can continually give to others. Jack Kornfield says, "There's a tremendous sorrow for a human being who doesn't find a way to give. One of the worst of human sufferings is not to find a way to love, or a place to work and give of your heart and your being (Brussat and Brussat 1996, 327)." An important way in which the older children in particular learned to give was through mentoring their younger buddies.

Just Watch Me Do This

Scattered throughout this book are examples of children mentoring one another—Jake and Tre demonstrating to David how to draw sea creatures and railroad tracks, Deana and Tati role-playing appropriate social behaviors, Sami showing her older buddies where the writing should go on the page they had just finished illustrating. As with the two of us, mentoring was a two-way process and a relationship that worked in both directions (see Chapter 5). In many respects, learning to be a mentor was a special kind of service for the buddies, specific to the immediate situation with peers. Through mentoring, the children acquired a sense of selflessness and learned to put themselves in the place of another. They grew as learners as they practiced teaching one another and felt a sense of accomplishment. At the end of the year, the first and second graders were asked as a homework assignment to list three things they did during the year that made them feel proud of themselves. Anna wrote: "We got the buddies to do the winter solstice even though they were a little wild at that time of year."

A Two-Way Street: Advantages of Children's Mentoring Relationships

- *It gives older children a chance to feel a sense of self-worth because they have helped a younger child.*
- *Younger children feel special because they receive attention from a child who is older and well-respected.*
- *Older children take pride in the younger child's accomplishments, feeling a part of the teaching/learning process.*
- *It gives teachers a handy way to keep unruly behavior in check. ("You wouldn't want your buddy to see you doing THAT, would you?")*
- *It's terrific training for future babysitters, teachers, and parents.*
- *It's a great way to pick up some wrestling moves from someone who has been at it a while longer.*

One unique aspect of the mentoring relationship for the first and second graders was the opportunity to practice the responsibilities that go with being a leader (Figure 4–2). Kelsey's mother wrote:

> *Kelsey loved having an older Seed as her buddy reader and looked forward to making her own contribution and meeting a new friend. Kelsey learned about authentic leadership from Travis . . . to listen, respect the individual, to appreciate and value his skills and abilities. She learned to be sensitive to someone else's needs and gained skills of patience, enthusiasm and care. She learned that there are differences in all of us and that they present unique challenges. Those challenges must always be looked at as opportunities to make a new friend and grow in the process.*

Throughout the year, the older children had many such opportunities as they learned to do the following:

- place the needs of others before their own
- make decisions based on prior and current knowledge
- plan educational choices with a specific outcome in mind
- generalize from a specific experience to a more general one
- make a difference in someone's life through an example of kindness
- understand what it means to have someone depending on you
- experience confidence and a feeling of success as a result of a job well done

We believe that this is one of the most significant outcomes of the buddy study, and one that will stay with the children for the remainder of their lives. The younger children were primarily the recipients of this special kind of service, but they too had the opportunity to learn to teach and give. The structure of the buddy arrangement and support of the relationships allowed for this to happen.

At the end of the school year, two pieces of writing appropriately summarized our year of collaboration. When the first and second graders were preparing their portfolios for conferences with their parents, Mary asked them to fill out a cover sheet to draw attention to their most significant work (Figure 4–3). In the section that began with "I am most proud of _____ because . . . ," Kelsey wrote: "I am most proud of math because I learned borrowing and caring." Although it is obvious within the context of her writing that she meant regrouping numbers for adding, or *carrying,* there was a strong message in what she actually wrote. It was a year of caring for everyone, and it was probably the most significant lesson we all took with us as the year came to an end.

FIGURE 4–2 *Kelsey, Melisa, and Travis*

During our school graduation ceremony, Julia was scrambling around searching for a scrap of paper. It was unclear what she was up to, until after the ceremony, when she approached Mary with this poem she wrote (Figure 4–4):

> The next time you cry bring a water bottle and drink your tears you will always store your friendship for we have not completely left each other we will make our hearts one

Julia's poem expressed her feelings about the school year coming to an end and about having to say good-bye to some of her classmates. It was also a fitting tribute to our buddy study. In nine short months, we accumulated enough memories to fill up cases of water bottles. And in the process, we all learned from one another how to be better human beings.

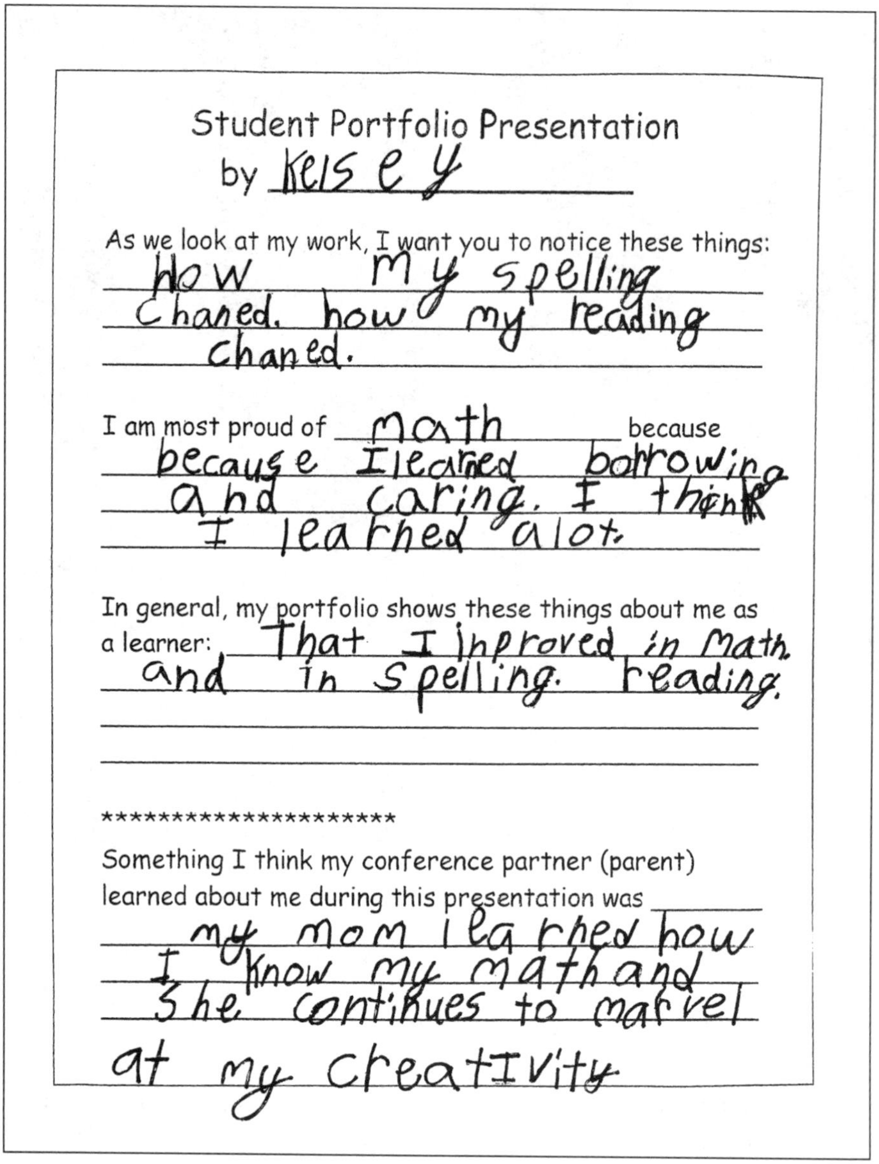

Student Portfolio Presentation
by Kelsey

As we look at my work, I want you to notice these things:
How my spelling chaned. how my reading chaned.

I am most proud of math because because I learned borrowing and caring. I think I learned a lot.

In general, my portfolio shows these things about me as a learner: That I inproved in math and in spelling. reading.

****

Something I think my conference partner (parent) learned about me during this presentation was _____
my mom learned how I know my math and she continues to marvel at my creativity

FIGURE 4–3 *Kelsey's Portfolio Page*

the next time you cry Bring A water Botlle And
Drink your tears You will Always store your fr
iendship for we Have not compleatly left each
Other we will makc Our Hearts one

Julia

FIGURE 4–4 *Julia's Poem/Graduation*

Five

Tenders of the Fire: Pedagogical Literacy

Writing this chapter proved to be quite a challenge. It was actually written three times, taking completely different forms each time. How do you take a year of learning for two teachers and condense it into a chapter that flows, is interesting, and is comprehensible? No story can be told without a beginning, Beth's English 101 teacher always said, so here you have it:

When Beth walked through the door of Awakening Seed for the first time for a teaching interview, she remembers being amazed. It was an early morning, before summer school began. A friendly teacher, whom she would later replace, greeted her with kindness and gave her directions for finding Mary. As she walked down the hallway, she looked at the walls of the school and peeked through the observation windows at each room. The walls were covered with paintings of children's favorite literary characters. Even the three-year-olds had participated and painted their own stick-figure likenesses on the wall. The classrooms were lined with children's work. No, they were wallpapered with it. Nowhere had Beth ever experienced a school that was so filled with the presence of children and their love of learning. Meeting Mary, discussing the school and

Beth's philosophy, and taking a tour only sealed the decision that had already been made in her mind—this was the place for her. Mary reported sensing immediately that Beth would be a perfect match for the Seed as well. From the very beginning, both felt that an extraordinary opportunity was about to unfold.

Many of the reasons for wanting to be at the Seed were exactly what created such a dynamic collaboration between us. There was, to be sure, an immediate kinship and friendship felt by both. We trusted one another's experience and work. We viewed our teaching lives similarly. For us, teaching was not a job (can it ever be just that if you are to be good?) but a way of life—a spiritual practice. As individual teachers, we valued critical pedagogy styles and theories. We both practiced reflective teaching. Praxis was a way of life already formed for us. In praxis, as described by Joan Wink in *Critical Pedagogy* (1997), teachers pause to reflect on their daily teaching practice. Through reflection and contemplation, these teachers gain insight into their practice. These insights sometimes result in theory transformation, which often causes the teacher to adapt classroom practices. Sometimes these insights result in affirmation and support for the current practice and ideas. Theory informs practice, which, through reflection, informs theory (Figure 5–1). Constant reflection allows practitioners to hone their daily teaching practice. For us, individually, the process is natural to who we are as teachers. Together, through collaboration, the process and our

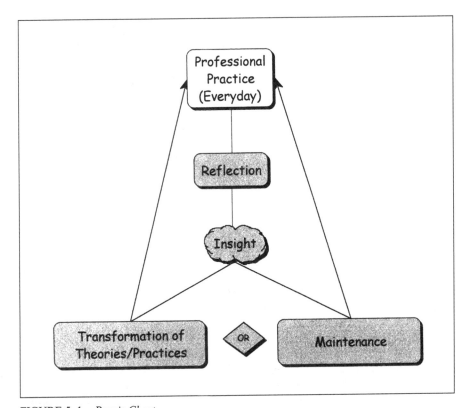

FIGURE 5–1   *Praxis Chart*

practice have been strengthened. Much of the strength is derived from these similarly held beliefs:

- Emergent curriculum is a valid and appropriate method of curriculum development.
- Taking a holistic approach to learning reaches the greatest number of students in the deepest ways.
- Good teaching involves listening closely to children and practicing critical pedagogy.
- Setting high standards for our students and ourselves elevates our work as teachers and learners.
- Collaboration holds the potential for arriving at greater insights than those we might discover on our own.

Shared Views

Emergent Curriculum

We hold a similar belief in an emergent form of curriculum building. These are some ways curriculum comes to life using this approach:

- by listening and taking notes about what the children discuss individually
- through attending to what they want to read
- by watching their fantasy play
- through whole-classroom discussions and brainstorming
- in response to world or local events or to special people in our lives
- due to a holiday or month devoted to a special purpose
- via literary responses
- as a result of a passion of an individual or a group
- through efforts to teach developmental tasks
- through daily routines, procedures, or rules

The train study, for example, was created through the infectious interest of one student from each of our classes. Curly-haired, bright-faced Antonio had a passion for trains that permeated every activity of the day. He often had a train on some part of his clothing, chose an electric train as his favorite character or animal of the day, and gave responses such as "Choo Choo!" when asked to give his favorite animal sound. One day Diane, the Spanish teacher, asked, "What does this make you think of?" She held up her fingers and wiggled them. Although Diane was hoping this prompt would remind them of "Diez Deditos," a frequently sung Spanish song about fingers, Antonio predictably raised his hand and said, "Trains!" Of course. In the weeks that followed, through Antonio, the other children became train enthusiasts as well by playing with him, reading books related to trains, playing with classroom toy trains, and asking him train questions.

When Not to Use Students' Ideas for a Class Study

- *if a topic is too broad (e.g., animals, the world)*
- *if a topic is too narrow (e.g., how a hummingbird builds its nest, types of motorcycles)*
- *if a topic is not age-appropriate (e.g., war equipment and scary creatures are not appropriate topics for three-year-olds)*
- *if only one child is interested in the topic (individual studies can be encouraged if a child is very passionate about a subject)*
- *if the topic relates only to the media, especially recent movies, cartoons, video games (e.g., Star Wars, Pokémon, Nintendo)*
- *if a child is echoing a parent's request, rather than an individual preference*

During one of our informal conversations, we were discussing the dynamics in our two classrooms, and Antonio's love of trains came up. As it turned out, Mike, a second grader, shared Antonio's infectious enthusiasm for trains. We remembered that he brought a model train to school one day earlier in the year. Mary mentioned that her father also shares the students' passion for trains and constructed an entire basement room in Nebraska dedicated to his model trains. Beth thought to herself, How can we *not* study trains at this point? She felt like she was standing on the tracks of her class, waiting to hear the low rumble of the approaching engine. As she waited, she put her hand on the tracks and lowered her ear to feel the vibration. As she did so, Beth felt, as much as heard, its arrival and welcomed it. To simply stay on the track—or ignore the noise and study something else she had chosen—would have been to ignore the children and to get hit by the oncoming train of their resistance or indifference. She knew nothing about trains, she thought. For her, a first-year teacher, there was a slight hesitation to embark on a journey to such an unfamiliar destination, but the train study with the buddy readers seemed to be scheduled in some far-off place, so when the train braked where we stood, everyone willingly climbed aboard. For both of us, and Beth in particular, the train study was our most significant experience of the year using the emergent curriculum approach. It revealed and confirmed other beliefs, especially those related to holistic teaching and learning.

Whole Teaching and Learning

Our shared belief about how children learn is one of the strongest elements of our educational perspective. We both take a holistic approach in our classrooms. We operate from the idea that children learn best when presented with quality literature, authentic and impactful experiences, and when given a voice in how the curriculum is formed. We believe that children need multiple and varied opportunities to express their knowledge and we both value the importance of questioning and challenging assumptions. Three-year-olds and second graders alike need experiences where they can be the expert, teach others what they know, and learn from one another (Figure 5–2) in respectful and supportive ways. The most important part of teaching for both of us is encouraging children to become compassionate, thoughtful, environmentally conscious human beings. This happens not only by attending to academic or cognitive issues but by addressing needs of the whole child through whole experiences. One student, for example, was dealing with the difficulties of a possible separation between his parents. We worked together to discuss the matter, recommend appropriate support services, and encourage participation in the preschoolers' class with a loved younger child going through a similar situation. We were able to closely monitor his progress academically, socially, and emotionally. Our holistic teaching practices are enhanced by careful observation, listening, and reflection.

Listening Deeply

Another common belief we hold is that teaching involves attending and listening in a deep way. Children should have a voice and be valued as individuals who bring something to the classroom, the school, and the community. This can hap-

FIGURE 5–2 *Taking Turns Being the Expert*

pen only if we make the time and effort to pay close attention to what they are saying and doing. In *Radical Presence*, Mary Rose O'Reilley (1998) describes a practice of deep listening between friends, which, over time, enables each person involved to pay attention in more profound ways. "True attention," she says, "invites us to change" (17). When we listen to our students in deep and clear ways, we can't help but respond to their needs and change our teaching practices more honestly and thoroughly.

Joan Wink (1997) discusses many aspects of teaching that we believe are important and related to deep listening. Critical pedagogy is best defined by what a practitioner does. A teacher practicing critical pedagogy is wide awake to his or her teaching. It is the process of looking at the education provided at small and large levels and seeing it clearly in all its many facets—processes, outcomes, power relationships, and professional and personal growth. It is being proactive in changing what we know doesn't work in the classroom and in education overall. Practicing critical pedagogy reignites the teacher's and the student's desire to learn. It keeps teaching fresh and combats burnout. It forces deep thought, reinforces the idea that anyone can and should ask and answer important questions, and challenges us to remember that we all take time to learn. Critical pedagogy is applicable to life, connects teachers and children to their imaginations, and pushes all involved to seek other views. It requires teachers to reexamine traditional assumptions and challenge them, and it invites us to pause, unlearn the outdated or ineffective, and relearn the practice every step of the way. It involves teaching based on theory, which is revised through the daily practice of teaching. Critical pedagogy allows us to review personal standards and expectations in the classroom and continually adjust them to meet both our students' needs and ours as teachers.

Setting High Standards

A common practice for the two of us is that of setting high standards for both ourselves and our students. We strive to do our best every day as teachers and expect the same from the children we teach. The classroom environments we create, individually and collaboratively, reflect these high standards. It is important to us that our students do their best and reach their highest potential as learners and human beings. We hold these same expectations for ourselves. Our work together has elevated our awareness of the importance of setting high standards, and our shared beliefs and standards contributed significantly to the importance and success of our collaborative efforts.

Working Together

The final shared view that contributed to the success of our work was the belief in the importance of collaboration. What happened in our collaboration far surpassed what was possible individually. Early on, we began to realize the extraordinary

> ## *Redefining Standards for Ourselves as Teachers*
>
> *In these days of standards set by those who think they know what is best for classroom teachers, it is crucial that we maintain our autonomy and reflect on what the idea of standards means for ourselves. Here are some thoughts we've had about standards:*
>
> - *We need to develop standards for ourselves, in addition to the imposed ones.*
> - *To keep standards high, we should keep our teaching fresh by continually learning new things alongside our students.*
> - *Continual dialogue with other teachers gives us support and a sense of unity to stand up for what we believe is right for children.*
> - *If we think of teaching as our lifework rather than a job, it helps us be more dedicated and invested in what we do every day.*
> - *Imposed standards don't have to be a bad thing; standards met through rich projects are more effective than those met through rote teaching.*
> - *Standards can be reframed as opportunities to extend and stretch the imaginations and minds of children, particularly if they are incorporated in natural, child-centered ways.*
> - *Our most important task as teachers is to keep what's best for children at the forefront of everything we do.*

experience and power of what was happening when we worked together. What follows is an examination of what we observed and learned from our year of collaboration.

Collaboration

A strong similarity in our philosophy and teaching style is our shared view of how curriculum is not only developed but is imparted to students. Traditional teaching involves seeing the teacher as a holder and transmitter of knowledge and the student as the receiver. For us, teaching is more of a transformational process. We learn alongside the children and hope that they are transformed into better people through the experiences in our classrooms.

> ### *Collaboration: What Made It Successful*
>
> - *sense of humor*
> - *shared love of coffee (we advise getting a frequent buyer's card)*
> - *similar passion for books, literature, and writing*
> - *shared quest for knowledge and deeper understanding*
> - *mutual level of commitment to children, to friendship, and to work*

In a collaboration between two reflective teachers, the possibilities are greatly expanded. Ruth Hubbard and Brenda Power (1999) write about "moments—the pulse points that define how teachers find a place for research in their lives" (34). In our work together, the pulse point came one day when we stood in Mary's classroom looking around at the students working together. We realized that there were many layers of learning happening simultaneously. It was not really a conscious decision but a reflex for both of us to take notes, document what was happening, and pay attention as closely as possible. We felt like we needed to get a clearer picture of the dynamics created when our classes were brought together, and it seemed most natural to work on it side by side.

We met on a regular basis, usually over coffee. Several significant things happened during these meetings. When reflecting on our work together, we were able to dig deeper. Every other week at first, and then more frequently later on, we were able to piece together the complexity we experienced with our classes. Our regular meetings enabled us to reflect upon our teaching practice, plan, and clarify our understanding of the experiences we were having in our own classrooms. It gave us a better picture of the children while they were together and of the learning experience of the two classes as a community. As a team, we were able to reconstruct events and make meaning of what transpired. This helped us fill in gaps for understanding particular children through background knowledge and observations, and we recounted the stories and events the students shared with us. We helped each other see what the other might have missed. The reflective component of our relationship was highly important to the success of our collaboration.

The reflection process for us included both conversation and written reflections in the form of anecdotal notes with quoted dialogue, e-mail correspondence, and writer's notebook entries. Our notebooks, storehouses of information, contain reflections about our teaching practice, idea webs, poems, writing anecdotes, connections between the world and the classroom, artifacts we find to be important, personal items, and clippings from articles (Figures 5–3, 5–4). This reflective process not only assisted us in uncovering the basis for content studies in the classroom but also allowed us to see patterns and gave us insight with which we were able to make better decisions about classroom setup, individual and community needs, scheduling, and necessary structure. This collaboration, paired with the attentive and reflective process, created a way for us to go deeper into our

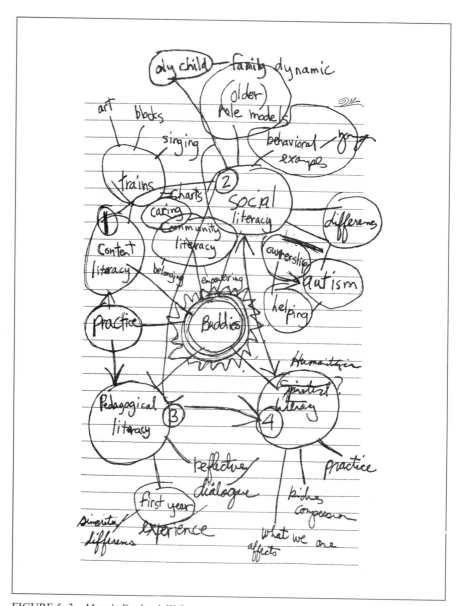

FIGURE 5–3 *Mary's Daybook Web*

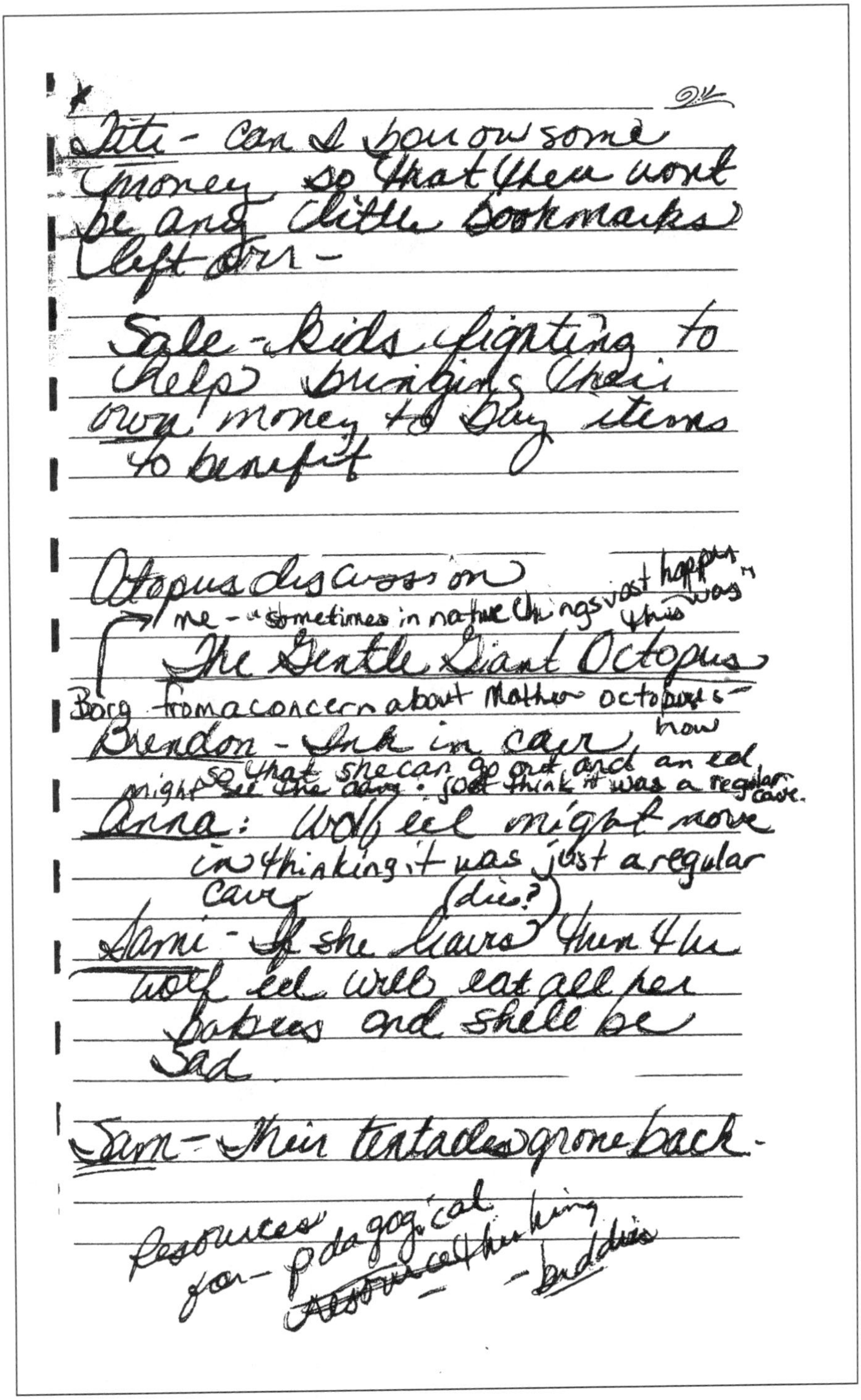

Titi - can I borrow some
money so that there won't
be any little bookmarks
left over -

Sale - Kids fighting to
help bringing their
own money to buy items
to benefit

Octopus discussion
me - "sometimes in nature things that happens this was"
  The Gentle Giant Octopus
Borg - from a concern about Mother octopus -
Brendon - Ink in cave, how
might so that she can go out and an eel
might see the cave. Just think it was a regular cave.
Anna: Wolf eel might move
  in thinking it was just a regular
  cave   (dies?)
Sami - If she leaves then the
  wolf eel will eat all her
  babies and she'll be
  sad

Sam - Their tentacles grow back -

resources for - pedagogical
thinking - buddies

FIGURE 5–4   *Beth's Daybook Notes*

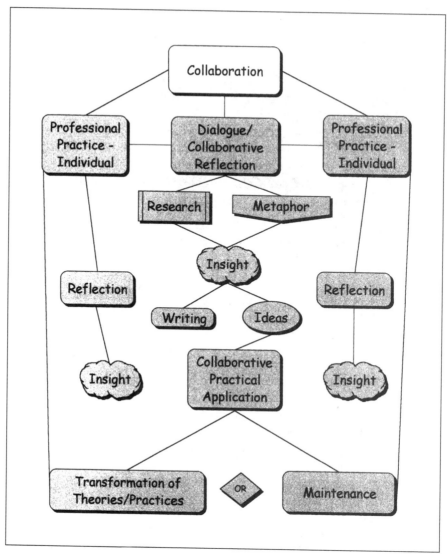

FIGURE 5–5 *Collaborative Praxis Chart*

work and also into ourselves as human beings (Figure 5–5). It allowed for a two-way mentoring relationship to develop.

Mentorship

We mentioned the value of the children's mentoring relationships in Chapter 4. The children were not the only ones to benefit from the mentoring process. Traditionally, such relationships between teachers are seen as beneficial primarily for the beginning teacher. They can aid in the growth and development of the novice during an often stressful transition from student to teacher (Veenman 1984). Ralph Fletcher (1993) discusses many characteristics of the mentor-novice relationship. His focus is on the writer and the student, but the ideas are the same. A mentor doesn't try to create a replica of him- or herself. A true mentor keeps "alive to the possibility of something new and distinctly original. A mentor possesses an inner honesty, an ability to recognize the novice's different style" (16). A mentor takes what works, even if difficult to find, and makes the novice aware of emerging skill. "Careful praise of this kind can fuel a writer [and a novice teacher] for a long time" (14). A mentor knows his or her trade and is respected by the novice, who is "becoming alive to the possibilities. . . . The mentor's high standards inspire the young writer [teacher] not to lower his or her own standards." Fletcher adds, "novices are deeply vulnerable to teachers' appraisals of their stories, poems, or essays. We must speak to our students with an honesty tempered by compassion: Our words will literally define the ways they perceive themselves as writers [teachers]" (19). Finally, he emphasizes the importance of tenderness over technique (18).

Mentoring as a Means of Moving Forward

Mentoring is a crucial part of teacher training and professional development. We have found these elements important for a successful mentoring relationship:

- *Remember it's a two-way relationship. Everyone has something to teach and learn, regardless of his or her level of experience or years in the profession.*

- *Preassigned pairings aren't always successful. The best mentoring relationships seem to happen naturally, with common interests, learning styles, personality qualities, and energy levels as the guiding influences.*

- *Competition should be avoided. A mentoring relationship thrives on encouragement, acknowledgment of successes, and celebration of growth by both the novice and the veteran on the team.*

- *If you're the more experienced person in the mentoring relationship, don't be surprised if your student surpasses you in many respects. If this happens, get out of the way and pat yourself on the back for a job well done.*

In our case, a successful mentor-novice relationship was inevitable. Beth, a beginning teacher, was excited to be working with Mary, a teacher for more than twenty years, a published writer, an experienced school director, and a holder of a master's degree. Beth also brought to the relationship a master's degree, as well as university teaching experience and experience in the business world. We soon found a strong friendship developing through our collaborative efforts. When we met, we met as friends, partners, mentor and novice, and researchers. Conversations were long and transforming as we explored the mentor relationship in new and inspiring ways. According to Fletcher (1993), a mentor truly should pass along everything he or she knows without strings attached. A mentor should make a student feel as though he or she is knowledgeable and should detach him- or herself from the need to compete or outdo the student. A true mentor takes pride in the accomplishments of the student and celebrates the day when he or she surpasses the mentor's own abilities. Mary embraced this mentor role. As in our lives with our children, there was never a sense of Mary simply transmitting information, but one of sharing ideas, experiences, and knowledge that had been passed on to her by her own wise mentors. We both sought the best learning as teachers and viewed the relationship as mutually beneficial.

A recent article discusses benefits for the mentor often not realized in mentor relationships. There is often a sense of pride and satisfaction for the mentor in contributing to the profession in general (Ackley and Gall 1992). Artie Voight once said to Ralph Fletcher, "It's such a great feeling to watch someone else enjoying what you love to do yourself" (Fletcher 1993, 18). Through the relationship with a novice, the mentor gets to experience the thrill of the craft—as well as its pain—all over again. In this way, the mentor's passion never gets spent; it gets renewed again and again through the mentoring relationship (Fletcher 1993).

For us, what happened between our classrooms stirred up fascination and enthusiasm to explore and reflect on what we were seeing. Digging deeper and making meaning of all that was happening allowed for the renewal of passion for teaching for both of us. This was an especially helpful process for Beth. She understood the concept of emergent curriculum very well in theory but didn't have much practical knowledge as a first-year teacher. As the school year began, she followed a carefully planned study of seeds. The class seemed to enjoy the study, but energy and passion always seemed to be missing. She realized that she was acting out of nervous tension and was planning activities that were not particularly relevant to the children in the class. When the train topic presented itself, she faced a great challenge. Her experience with trains amounted to walking along train tracks and bridges as a child and seeing the trains pass by. It was a bit scary for her to embark on a journey so foreign. The environment of the school, the quiet support of her teaching philosophy, the trust placed in her efforts to try new ideas, and the knowledge that she would be sustained by a strong mentoring relationship gave her the courage to move forward.

Mentoring was a rewarding, unintentional consequence of our collaborative buddy study. It was informal and was woven into the fabric of and emerged from our conversations and experiences with our classes. The mentoring relationship emerged just like the curriculum; in a sense, it was the curriculum for our teaching journey. For Beth, the results were a greater confidence in her teaching life and the realization that teaching is a continual process. For Mary, it was a reminder that even after more than twenty years of experience, there is still much to be learned and lived in a teaching life. It was additionally gratifying for her to know that the work she'd devoted her entire life to would continue through the work of another human being. Knowing she'd had at least a small part in furthering the work of another teacher was important. She also realized it's a way to give or pass along what has been bestowed by others. Having a worthy student is a most gratifying experience for a mentor.

Learning from each other extended to writing this story. Beth, a novice writer, began to learn how to see herself as a writer. After the first draft of each chapter, we exchanged pages and offered suggestions. We then met to go over the chapters. When the discussion turned to this chapter, there was tension in the air as we explored possible changes. It was the first time in over a year of working together that any kind of tension was present between us. Beth envisioned detailed editing written on the pages, which would help for future revisions. Mary suggested rearranging and rewriting the chapter. She pushed Beth to extend herself as a writer. The experience led to a pause in the writing of this book as well as a reflection for both of us. For Beth, there was a close examination of what it means to be a writer, how to ask for exactly what you want and need from an editor, and how to take constructive suggestions about your writing. For Mary, it was a significant lesson in mentoring fledgling writers.

We set aside the writing for a number of reasons, not the least of which was to give ourselves a space in which to reflect on how our collaboration was being affected by the process of trying to put it into written form. We realized that, as with children, the important lessons in life can't be forced or rushed. We needed to give ourselves time to let the big ideas germinate and to find a way to articulate them. What eventually drew us back to the writing was our belief in the importance of sharing our research with others. We were encouraged by others to make our research available to teachers who might not have the good fortune of having someone with whom to work as we did. Our belief in the power of collaboration and the significance of teachers using their voices energized us once again. We felt obligated to finish telling our story and at the same time offer an invitation to other teachers, alone and in collaboration, to initiate their own research studies.

For both of us, underlying our educational assumptions and beliefs is the desire to be one of those special teachers whom children will remember throughout their lives. We wish to be remembered for everything the children have experienced and take with them as a result of living in our classrooms. Complementary to that is our belief in a reflective practice. Wanting to be the best we can be for children and approaching teaching reflectively certainly inspired us to examine our practice more rigorously. But there was something else that moved us to take ourselves more seriously as teacher researchers. As the year went by, we realized that what we were experiencing was important. We saw in its complexity some keys for successful, rewarding teaching, which we believed might be of benefit to other teachers, too. Once we started organizing our observations into the different layers of literacy, the idea to document the process naturally followed. As we documented our work and reflected upon it, our teaching practices were elevated. The insights we gained from our research brought more questions and answers and, ultimately, better teaching. Knowing how much this process helped us, we believed that it was a story worth telling.

Today's teacher is responsible for so many different areas of a child's development. There is a call for teachers who have a caring heart and a critical eye (Wink 1997). An exceptional teacher must see the big picture in order to improve the lives of the children in the classroom and, in fact, the community all around. There is a charge to send children out into the world with minds capable of seeking other ways of understanding, of looking critically at the world around them and feeling empowered to make changes in a compassionate manner. Children are asked to be problem solvers but are often not given much real opportunity to practice this in school. Rarely are teachers given a chance to be problem solvers, especially when curriculum is mandated from the top down. Teacher researchers can address these important issues.

"We look for that elusive edge—between comfortable, old teaching methods and prickly new research strategies—that teachers traverse all the time when they wrestle with finding a place for inquiry in their lives" (Hubbard and Power 1999, 34). A teacher researcher seeks to understand the elements that make up his or her practice, the issues affecting the practice, and the environment in which the practice takes place. The goal of most teacher researchers is to understand and respond through their teaching practice in ways that will enable their students to learn more effectively. The teacher researcher's world—and work—is one of questions and one of change based on inquiry, or as Goodlad said when reflecting on the words of John Dewey, "What the researcher in education must do is to get immersed in the complex phenomena, then withdraw and think about the issues" (Goldberg 1995, 85).

I Don't Have Time to Do Research!: How to Begin

Writing a book or article needn't always be the goal of research. You may want to do research simply to reflect, refine your practice, or see things in a new way.

- *Start simply. You can begin with a study of one individual in your class, a specific part of the day, or a study you are doing. You can begin with a question you want to answer (e.g., What can I do to get the children better settled for math?) or simply record information because it seems important and you want to revisit it later for further development.*

- *Use any available tool. We like sticky notes, charts, webs, journals, e-mail writing, dialogue, and copies of the children's work for documentation. You can simply record discussions (video or audio) and review them later for important information.*

- *Open your journal or daybook and leave it open in an area you can get to frequently during the day. Write when you can.*

- *Take a few minutes daily to reflect on and write about anything that seems important or has made an impact on you.*

- *Work with someone else, talk through methods and ideas, discuss possibilities.*

- *Read research whenever possible. It can spark interest and bring up pertinent questions.*

- *Attend conferences. Being in the presence of leaders in the field is inspiring and keeps you current with the pulse of the teacher research community.*

Teacher research is not always seen in a positive light. "Teacher research is organic, sometimes messy, unpredictable, and generative, just like teachers' lives in and out of school" (Patterson et al. 1993, 9). Seen as "imperfect researchers" (Applebee 1987), teachers are thought to be too closely tied to the subjects they are studying. There are often questions of detachment and rigor. Some believe that only data derived from studies set up using out-of-context experimental designs are worth consideration. Many of these studies rely on objective, quantifiable events. They focus on correlation and experimental examination of effective teaching behavior. What is important is what the observable behavior means, rather than the participant's lived experience. Wink (1997) writes:

We are not to be passive, robotic technocrats who can't do anything because of the administration, or the texts, or the parents, or the students, or the tests. We are to be intellectuals and professionals who take control of our own teaching and learning. Perhaps we can't control society's perception of teachers as less, but we can control how we perceive ourselves. My suspicion is that as we begin to come to know ourselves as intellectuals and professionals, and turn those beliefs into behaviors, society will begin to change its perception of us. (92)

A basis of holistic teaching is that the whole is greater than the sum of its parts. When doing research in a holistic classroom, then, one must be a fully present participant to truly understand the nature of the classroom (Goodman 1989). "The researcher must personally become situated in the natural setting and study first hand over a prolonged period of time the object of interest and the various contextual features that influence it" (Smith 1987, 175). Only a teacher, then, can best study his or her classroom. He or she has the contextual understanding necessary to fully comprehend what's taking place. A community of teacher researchers can provide rich information that serves the teaching community and policy makers. Teacher researchers will also add professionalism to the teaching field and create a knowledge bank that is relevant to other practitioners.

Our journey is told within these pages. It is our challenge to every teacher that you do research in your classroom. Look closely and reflectively at your teaching practice. Review, revise, and write if you can. Find another teacher who holds similar or complementary interests and begin a dialogue. It is this sort of practice that keeps the candle of hope burning in schools. It keeps love for the profession possible in a climate of change, pressure, high-stakes testing, and standards. We believe that as teachers it is important to tell our specific stories of research and classroom life, not only to bring much-needed acknowledgment and respect to the profession but also to enable other teachers to see a larger picture through a single case study (Brown 1999). We invite you to ask questions, follow your intuition, conduct your own research studies, and take the chance that you may arrive at a new place of understanding that will enrich your life and the lives of the children you teach.

References

Ackley, B., and M. Gall. 1992. "Skills, Strategies, and Outcomes of Successful Mentor Teachers." Paper presented at the annual meeting of the American Educational Research Association. San Francisco.

Albom, M. 1997. *Tuesdays with Morrie*. New York: Doubleday.

Applebee, A. 1987. "Musings: Teachers and the Process of Research." *Research in the Teaching of English* 21: 5–7.

Bolster, A. S. 1983. "Toward a More Effective Model of Research on Teaching." *Harvard Educational Review* 53 (3): 294–308.

Brown, J. 1999. "We Have Met the Audience and She Is Us: The Evolution of Teacher as Audience for Research." In *Living the Questions*, ed. R. Hubbard and B. Power. York, ME: Stenhouse.

Brownell, C. A. 1990. "Peer Social Skills in Toddlers: Competencies and Constraints Illustrated by Same-Age and Mixed-Age Interaction." *Child Development* 61 (3): 38–48.

Brussat, F. and M. A. Brussat. 1996. *Spiritual Literacy*. New York: Scribner.

Bunting, E. 1996. *Train to Somewhere*. New York: Clarion.

Crews, D. 1992. *Freight Train*. New York: Mulberry.

Das, S. 1997. *Awakening the Buddha Within*. New York: Broadway.

———. 1999. *Awakening to the Sacred: Creating a Spritual Life from Scratch*. New York: Broadway.

Fletcher, R. 1993. *What a Writer Needs*. Portsmouth, NH: Heinemann.

French, D. C., et al. 1986. "Leadership Asymmetries in Mixed Age Children's Groups." *Child Development* 57 (5): 1277–83.

Fry, T., OSB. ed. 1982. *RB 1980: The Rule of St. Benedict*. Collegeville, MN: Liturgical.

Glover, M. 1997. *Making School by Hand*. Urbana, IL: National Council of Teachers of English.

Goldberg, M. 1995. "Portrait of John Goodlad." *Educational Leadership* 52 (6): 82–85.

Goodman, K. 1989. "Whole-Language Research: Foundations and Development." *The Elementary School Journal* 90 (2): 207–19.

Hubbard, R., and B. Power. 1999. "Becoming Teacher Researchers One Moment at a Time." *Language Arts* 7 (1): 34–39.

Hughes, L. 1994. *The Dream Keeper and Other Poems*. New York: Alfred A. Knopf.

Jones, E., and J. Nimmo. 1993–1994. *Emergent Curriculum*. Washington, D.C.: National Association for the Education of Young Children.

Kirby, K. 1989. "Community Service and Civic Education." *ERIC Digest*. 31 May 2000. *http://www.ed.gov/databases/ERIC_Digests/ed309135.html*.

Lawrence, J. 1995. *The Great Migration: An American Story*. New York: HarperTrophy.

MacLachlan, P. 1993. *Baby*. New York: Bantam Doubleday Dell.

Merriam-Webster OnLine Dictionary. 10 August 1999. *http://www.m-w.com/dictionary*.

Merton, T. 1961. *New Seeds of Contemplation*. New York: New Directions.

Moore, L. 1969. "Winter Dark." *I Thought I Heard the City*. New York: Atheneum.

O'Reilley, M. R. 1998. *Radical Presence*. Portsmouth, NH: Boynton/Cook.

Patterson, L., C. Santa, K. Short, and K. Smith. 1993. *Teachers Are Researchers: Reflection and Action*. Newark, DE: International Reading Association.

Peterson, R. 1992. *Life in a Crowded Place*. Portsmouth, NH: Heinemann.

Project Wild. 1994. *Aquatic Project Wild*. Bethesda, MD: Western Regional Environmental Education Council.

Reynolds, M. 1984. *Morningtown Ride*. Freedom, CA: Crossing.

Seuss, Dr. 1957. *The Cat in the Hat*. New York: Random House.

Smith, M. 1987. "Publishing Qualitative Research." *American Educational Research Journal*. Summer 24 (2): 173–83.

Stone, S. 1998. "Creating Contexts for Mixed-Age Learning." *Childhood Education* 74 (4): 234–36.

Tauer, S. M. 1996. "The Mentor-Protogé Relationship and Its Effects on the Experienced Teacher." Paper presented at the annual conference of the American Educational Research Association. April 8–12. New York.

Veenman, S. 1984. "Perceived Problems of Beginning Teachers." *Review of Educational Research* 54 (2): 143–78.

Wallace, K. 1998. *Gentle Giant Octopus*. Cambridge, MA: Candlewick.

Wink, J. 1997. *Critical Pedagogy: Notes from the Real World*. White Plains, NY: Longman.

Books About Autism

Gerlach, E. 1999. *Just This Side of Normal: Glimpses into Life With Autism.* Eugene, OR: Four Leaf Press.

Grandin, T. 1996. *Thinking in Pictures: And Other Reports from My Life With Autism.* New York: Vintage Books.

————. 1996. *Emergence: Labeled Autistic.* New York: Warner Books.

Harris, S., and M. Weiss. 1998. *Right From the Start: Behavioral Intervention for Young Children With Autism: A Guide for Parents and Professionals.* Bethesda, MD: Woodbine House.

Koegel, R., and L. Koegel. 1998. *Teaching Children With Autism: Strategies for Initiating Positive Interactions and Improving Learning Opportunities.* Baltimore, MD: Paul Brookes.

Kozloff, M. 1998. *Reaching the Autistic Child: A Parent Training Program.* Cambridge, MA: Brookline Books.

Maurice, C. 1993. *Let Me Hear Your Voice: A Family's Triumph over Autism.* New York: Fawcett Columbine.

Maurice, C., S. Luce, and G. Green. eds. 1996. *Behavioral Intervention for Young Children With Autism: A Manual for Parents and Professionals.* Austin, TX: PRO-ED.

Powers, M. ed. 1989. *Children With Autism: A Parent's Guide.* Bethesda, MD: Woodbine House.

Seroussi, K., and B. Rimland. 2000. *Unraveling the Mystery of Autism and Pervasive Developmental Disorder: A Mother's Story of Research and Recovery.* New York: Simon and Schuster.

Children's Titles

Amenta, C. 1992. *Russell Is Extra Special: A Book About Autism for Children.* Washington, D.C.: American Psychology Association.

Brown, T. 1984. *Someone Special Just Like You.* New York: Henry Holt.

Katz, I. et al. 1993. *Joey and Sam: A Heartwarming Storybook About Autism, a Family, and a Brother's Love.* Los Angeles: Real Life Storybooks.

Lears, L. 1998. *Ian's Walk: A Story About Autism.* Grove, IL: Albert Whitman and Co.

Senisi, E. 1998. *Just Kids: Visiting a Class for Children with Special Needs.* New York: Dutton.

Thompson, M. 1996. *Andy and His Yellow Frisbee.* Bethesda, MD: Woodbine House.

Watson, E. 1996. *Talking to Angels.* New York: Harcourt.

Index

collaboration and, 84, 86
forms of, 83–84
teacher research and, 90–92
by teachers, 83–86
research studies, 3. *See also* teacher research
reading, 91
by teachers, 90–92
writing and, 89
responsibility
building community through, 57–59
for dance performance, 58
mentoring and, 72
need for, 57
risk taking
buddy bubbles and, 3
collaboration and, 40
rituals
community building through, 51–52
singing as, 52–53
value of, 52
Rivera, Diego, 23
rock salt, for ice sculpture project, 21
role models
development of, 34–36
problem solving and, 42
promoting, 35
social relationships and, 34
student image as, 44
value of, 36
role playing, conflict resolution through, 37–38
routines
community building through, 51–52
value of, 52
Ruby (elephant), 48
Rules of St. Benedict (Fry), 55

sand, for Mud and Sand Day activities, 31, 33
school service projects, 79
seed study, 88
self-esteem
community service projects and, 70–71
through community projects, 56
service
community service projects, 69–71
understanding, 69
Seuss, Dr., 63–64
shared history, community building through, 51
shared knowledge, community building through, 52
sibling-like relationships, among reading buddies, 48–49
sibling rivalry, among reading buddies, 48
singing
community building through, 3
in nursing home, 67
as ritual, 52–53

students with autism and, 64
train songs, 5, 13, 15
sleeping bag sewing project, 56
socialization skills, 48
social learning
in preschool, 35–46
social relationships and, 39
social literacy, 34–45
defined, 6
social relationships
among buddies, 34
buddy reading and, 38–39
as extended family, 47–50
poetry of appreciation about, 44
reflections on, in student logs, 44
reflective conversations about, 42
role models, 34–36
social learning and, 39
touching and, 38
"Special Pair, The," 44
standards
importance of, 78, 81
for teachers, 82
states of matter
changing, 18–22
homework, 18–19
ice sculpture project, 18–22
stationery, for ocean study project, 1, 28
student ideas, for emergent curriculum, 78–79
student log entries
on block trains, 13
on buddy relationships, 44
on Earth model, 29
on personal growth, 40–41
on train ABC book project, 11–12
student teachers
celebrations, 56
going away party for, 54–55
Sweet Honey in the Rock, 23

tactile sensation, 33
teacher research, 90–92. *See also* research studies
beginning, 91
criticism of, 91
goal of, 90
holistic teaching and, 92
reflection and, 90, 92
tools for, 91
value of, 90, 92
writing and, 89
teachers
collaboration by, 77–78, 81–86
listening deeply by, 78, 80–81
problem solving by, 90
redefining standards for, 82
student relationships with, 48